The Kids' Around the World Cookbook

Copyright © McRae Books Srl 2004

This edition published 2006 in the United Kingdom by
A & C Black Publishers Ltd, 36 Soho Square, London W1D 3QY
www.acblack.com
Reprinted 2006, 2009

Published by permission of McRae Books Srl, Borgo S. Croce, 8 – Florence, Italy.
ISBN-13: 978-0-7136-7847-5

A CIP catalogue record for this book is available from the British Library.

McRae Books Srl
Project Manager: Anne McRae
Texts: Rosalba Gioffré, Frances Lee, Karen Ward
Editor: Alison Wilson, Helen Farrell
Photography: Marco Lanza, Walter Mericchi
Set Design: Rosalba Gioffrè
Design: Marco Nardi
Layout and cutouts: Ornella Fassio, Adriano Nardi, Giovanni Mattioli,
Sebastiano Ranchetti
Special thanks to: Mastrociliegia (Fiesole) and Dino Bartolini (Florence),
who kindly lent props for photography
Colour separations: Fotolito Toscana, Florence, Italy
Printed in China

The Kids' Around the World Cookbook

A & C Black • London

Introduction

This book has 56 recipes for easy-to-prepare dishes that young chefs will enjoy preparing as much as they will love eating them! We have chosen the recipes our own children like best from all around the world. There are lots of scrumptious Italian dishes and many French favourites, but you will also find recipes from China, Mexico, the United States, Austria, India, New Zealand, Singapore, Canada and more. So, Happy Cooking and... ENJOY!

Safety in the Kitchen

The recipes in this book were developed by three young mothers who are aware of the precautions required when cooking with young children. All the recipes have been tested with children and are suitable for those aged 8 and up. However, an adult must stay in the kitchen and supervise children at all times whilst they are cooking. Many pages have a 'Tips & Tricks' box with safety suggestions for young chefs, such as asking an adult to help lift pans of boiling water or remove heavy dishes from the oven. Teach children good hygiene practices in the kitchen. Always wash your hands before and after handling food, and before eating. Keep food covered and store it correctly, e.g. in a refridgerator.

Tomato and Basil Toasts

This delicious snack comes from Italy, where it is served throughout the summer when tomatoes are tasty and plentiful. In Italian, these toasts are called *bruschetta*. Remember to pronounce the word as "brusketta," because in Italian the letters "ch" have a hard sound, as in the English word "architect."

6

Ingredients

2 thick slices heavy white bakery bread

2 cloves garlic, peeled

6 fresh basil leaves

2 tablespoons extra virgin olive oil

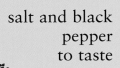

salt and black pepper to taste

2 large ripe salad tomatoes

Rinse your fingertips in a little vinegar to eliminate the strong smell of garlic.

1 Toast the bread until light golden brown. Rub each slice with a clove of garlic. The crispy surface of the toast will "grate" the garlic and quickly absorb it.

Utensils

CUTTING BOARD

KNIFE

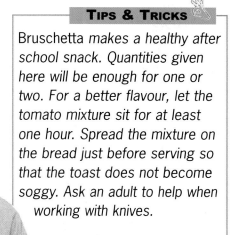

2 Rinse the tomatoes and wipe them dry with paper towels. Chop the tomatoes into cubes and spread them over the toast. Take special care with the knife. You do not need a very sharp one. An ordinary bread knife is fine.

TIPS & TRICKS

Bruschetta *makes a healthy after school snack. Quantities given here will be enough for one or two. For a better flavour, let the tomato mixture sit for at least one hour. Spread the mixture on the bread just before serving so that the toast does not become soggy. Ask an adult to help when working with knives.*

3 Rinse the basil and shake lightly until dry. Use your fingertips to tear the basil into pieces and sprinkle it over the tomatoes. Season with a little salt.

4 Drizzle the *bruschetta* with olive oil to taste. If you like spicy food, sprinkle a little black pepper over the top.

Hot Mexican Salsa

"Caliente!" means "hot!" in Spanish. That is the best way to describe this famous sauce. *Salsa* is a mixture of tomatoes, onions, chillies, and other ingredients. *Salsa* is served all over Mexico with tortillas and grilled meats, fish, or rice. It is also a popular starter and is served with a bowl of tortilla chips. This dish is best made during the hot summer months, when tomatoes are really ripe.

The inside veins and seeds of a jalapeno chilli are very hot. If possible, wear rubber gloves when chopping them. Make sure you do not rub your eyes, and wash your hands with soap after handling the chillies.

1 Chop the onion, coriander, and tomatoes. Place them in a small bowl.

2 Finely chop the chilli and add it to the bowl. Do not touch your eyes!

Utensils

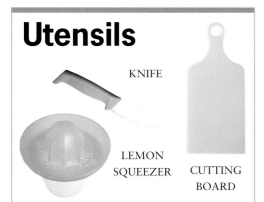

KNIFE

LEMON SQUEEZER

CUTTING BOARD

TIPS & TRICKS

Always wash your hands before you start to cook. When using fruit and vegetables, always rinse them under cold running water before cutting them. Washing the food removes harmful pesticides. Even fruit of which you normally only use the insides, such as lemons or limes, should be rinsed before use.

3 Squeeze the limes, then pour the juice into the bowl with the tomatoes. Be careful to remove the lime pips, which are very bitter. Add the salt and mix well.

4 Place the salsa in a serving dish. Serve with tortilla chips or as a sauce. It will taste best if made a day in advance.

Ingredients

1 onion

1 bunch coriander

2 tomatoes

1 large chilli

3 limes

½ teaspoon salt

Toasted Cheese and Ham Sandwich

This toasted sandwich, known in French as a "*croque-monsieur*," comes from Paris, France, where it was invented in a bar on the Boulevard des Capucines in 1910. A sort of French fast food, you can make a number of variations of this sandwich. Try topping it with a fried egg. In this case it is called a "*croque-madame*!"

1 Preheat the oven to 180°C/ 350°F/gas 4. Leave the butter to soften at room temperature. It should be soft but not melted. Use a spatula or bread knife to spread it onto one side of the bread.

2 Grate the cheese. Be sure to keep your fingertips well away from the grater.

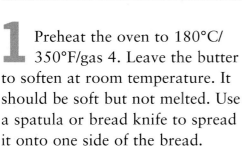

TIPS & TRICKS

Ask an adult to help you when putting the sandwich into, or taking it out of the oven. If you do it yourself, be sure to wear thick oven gloves to protect your hands.

Ingredients

1 tablespoon butter

2 slices bread

30 g (1 oz) gruyère or Swiss cheese

2 slices ham

3 Cover one of the slices of bread with two slices of ham. Trim off any extra ham and place it in the middle. Sprinkle the grated cheese over the ham.

When you add the cheese, place most of it in the centre of the sandwich to stop it from coming out when cooking.

Utensils

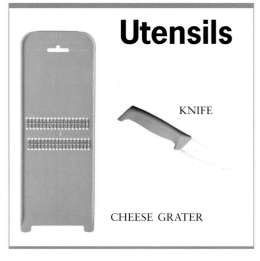

KNIFE

CHEESE GRATER

4 Place the other slice of bread on top, with the buttered side facing inward. Cook the sandwich in the oven for about 15 minutes, or until nicely browned.

Chicken Liver Toasts

Don't be put off by some of the ingredients in this recipe. The chicken livers and anchovies mix in with the other ingredients to make a delicious topping for the toast. This is another Italian dish. It is found all over Italy, but originally comes from Tuscany, where it is served as an *"antipasto"* (appetiser) along with a platter of ham and salami.

Ingredients

300 g (10 oz) chicken livers, cleaned and fat removed

2 anchovies (from a tin, preserved in oil)

2 tablespoons capers

salt (taste first, the anchovies and capers are already salty)

1 small red onion, coarsely chopped

4 tablespoons extra virgin olive oil

1 baguette (French loaf)

TIPS & TRICKS

You will need a sharp knife to chop the chicken livers and onion. Be very careful while doing this. Hold the knife well up the handle and keep your fingers away from the blade. Ask an adult to help. Junior cooks in Italy use a 'half-moon' chopper, because they are much safer.

1 Use a bread knife with a serrated blade to slice the bread into rounds about 1 cm (½ inch) thick and toast lightly.

Utensils

HALF-MOON
CHOPPER

CUTTING
BOARD

FOOD MILL

FRYING
PAN

2 Rinse the chicken livers and chop coarsely. Cook in a frying pan over a high heat for 1 minute. Then add the oil, onion, anchovies, and capers. Cook for 3–4 minutes. With an adult's help, pour in 125 ml (¼ pint) hot water, and cook for 8–10 more minutes.

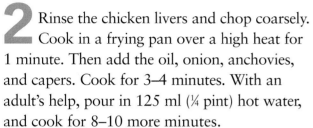

3 Taste the mixture to see if it needs salt. Remove the pan from the heat and put the mixture into a food processor with 2 tablespoons of warm water. Blend until creamy.

4 Spread the mixture on the toasted bread. Arrange on a dish and serve.

Guacamole

Guacamole is a Mexican dip made of mashed avocados. It is flavoured with chillies and lime or lemon juice, and often has chopped tomatoes, spring onion and coriander. The word *"guacamole"* comes from two Aztec words – *"agucate"* meaning "avocado," and *"mole"* meaning "mixture." Some Mexican cities have their own way of serving *guacamole*. In Monterrey, the tomatoes and onions are served as a garnish, so that the dish looks like the red, white, and green stripes on the Mexican flag.

1 Cut the avocados in half lengthwise. Remove the stones.

2 Use a spoon to hollow out the green, fleshy part of the avocados. Put the flesh into a bowl.

TIPS & TRICKS

Many recipes in this book involve the use of a sharp knife for chopping and cutting ingredients. Take care when choosing the knife. Talk to an adult about which is the best and safest knife in your kitchen for each job. When using a knife, hold it firmly in one hand and hold the ingredient in the other. Make sure that your fingers are well away from the blade.

3 Mash the avocado flesh using a fork. Add the lemon or lime juice and salt. Stir.

4 Chop the spring onions and the chillies. Peel and mince the garlic. Add all of them to the mashed avocado and stir well.

5 Chop the tomato into small pieces. Add the pieces to the avocado and stir well.

Utensils

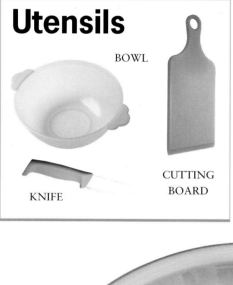

BOWL

KNIFE

CUTTING BOARD

6 Place the guacamole in an attractive serving dish. Serve with tostados, or tortilla chips, as a dip.

Ingredients

2 avocados

½ teaspoon salt

2 teaspoons lemon or lime juice

1 small tomato

2 cloves garlic

1 spring onion

2 green chillies

Tacos

Tacos make a tasty lunch or snack. You can prepare the fillings in advance. Make sure you fill the taco shells just before serving so that they stay crunchy. Add Hot Mexican Salsa (pages 8–9) to your tacos for extra flavour. Taco filling also tastes great on top of a *chalupa*. To make a *chalupa*, fry a tortilla flat instead of in a curved pocket.

Utensils

WOODEN SPOON

SAUCEPAN

CUTTING BOARD

KNIFE

FRYING PAN

Ingredients

1 small onion

2 ripe tomatoes

1 lettuce, washed and chopped

1–2 cloves garlic

500 g (1 lb) ground (minced) beef

1 teaspoon salt

1 teaspoon chilli powder (optional)

10 to 12 hard taco shells

250 g (8 oz) cooked beans drained, or refried beans

375 g (12 oz) cheddar cheese, grated

1 Chop the onion, tomatoes, lettuce, and garlic and set them aside.

2 Place a frying pan over medium heat. Add the beef, garlic, salt, and chilli powder to the pan. If you are using cooked beans, add these to the pan as well. Cook and stir until the meat is brown. Make sure there is no pink left in the meat. Drain away any liquid from the meat.

TIPS & TRICKS

If you cannot find crunchy taco shells, ask an adult to make them for you. Heat some oil in a frying pan. Place a corn tortilla in the hot oil. Use tongs to fold it over. Fry one side and then the other. Drain the shells on kitchen roll.

3 Fill the taco shells with meat, beans, lettuce, tomato, and onion.

4 Top with grated cheddar cheese. If you like, you can also add spoonfuls of spicy *salsa*.

Spring Rolls

Spring rolls are a favourite starter, and they are not too difficult to make at home. They can be made in advance and kept in the fridge until you are ready to cook them. You can change the filling to suit your own tastes.

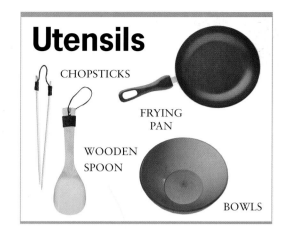

Utensils

CHOPSTICKS

FRYING PAN

WOODEN SPOON

BOWLS

1 Place a large frying pan over high heat. Add 2 tablespoons of oil. Stir fry the turnip or cabbage and the carrots until lightly cooked.

2 Add the water chestnuts and bamboo shoots to the pan and stir until they are heated.

3 Add the shrimps, sugar, soy sauce, salt and pepper to the pan and mix well. Pour the mixture into a large bowl and leave to cool.

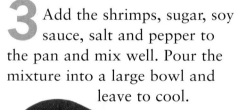

TIPS & TRICKS

Spring rolls must be fried in hot oil to be crispy. If the oil is not hot enough the rolls will be soggy. If it is too hot, the rolls will burn. To test if the oil is hot enough, take a bit of bread and put it in the oil. If the bread sizzles and browns, the oil is hot enough. Boiling oil can splatter and cause nasty burns. Never use it to fry anything unless an adult helps you.

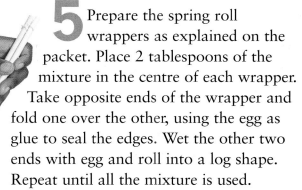

5 Prepare the spring roll wrappers as explained on the packet. Place 2 tablespoons of the mixture in the centre of each wrapper. Take opposite ends of the wrapper and fold one over the other, using the egg as glue to seal the edges. Wet the other two ends with egg and roll into a log shape. Repeat until all the mixture is used.

4 Crack open the egg and beat it in a small bowl using chopsticks or a fork.

6 Heat the remaining oil in a deep pan until very hot. Slip the spring rolls into the oil and fry until golden brown, turning frequently so that they brown evenly all over.

7 Using a slotted spoon, remove the cooked rolls from the pan and place on paper towels to absorb the extra oil. Serve hot.

Ingredients

1 litre (2 pints) vegetable oil

250 g (8 oz) shredded turnip or green cabbage

250 g (8 oz) shredded carrot

1 small tin shredded bamboo shoots

60 g (2 oz) diced water chestnuts

125 g (4 oz) diced cooked shrimps.

pinch of sugar

2 tablespoons soy sauce

1 egg

salt and pepper to taste

1 packet of rice paper wrappers

Pakoras

Vegetables fried in crispy batter, called pakoras, are a favourite food at Holi celebrations in northern India. Holi, which is held in February or March to celebrate the end of winter, is one of the liveliest celebrations in the Hindu year. If you like ketchup, serve these tasty fritters with a bowl of ketchup on the side.

Utensils

FRYING PAN

BOWL

SLOTTED SPATULA

1 Mix the flour, salt, and spices in a large bowl.

2 Add 2 tablespoons of oil and the herbs and stir to make a thick batter. Let stand for 30 minutes.

TIPS & TRICKS

Hot oil can cause nasty burns. See the Tips & Tricks box on page 18 for advice on how to fry safely. Always ask an adult to help you.

Ingredients

200 g (7 oz) plain flour

1 teaspoon each of salt, ground cumin, ground coriander seed, chilli powder, turmeric

2 tablespoons oil + more for frying

180 ml (⅓ pint) water

bunch of fresh mint leaves

1 tablespoon poppy seeds

500 g (1 lb) mixed vegetables

3 Cut the vegetables into thick slices and dip into the batter.

4 Heat the oil in a deep frying pan or a deep fat fryer until very hot.

5 Add the vegetables in small batches.

6 Fry for 4–6 minutes, or until golden brown and crispy all over. Drain well on paper towels and serve hot.

Shrimp and Pork Dim Sum

These little dumplings are a classic *dim sum* dish. In Cantonese cuisine, dim sum is usually served as an early lunch. A dim sum meal consists of a variety of steamed and deep-fried items, such as dumplings and mini spring rolls, and ends with custard tarts.

Utensils

LARGE BOWL

WOODEN SPOON

GRATER

STEAMER

LARGE WOK

1 Combine all the ingredients, except the wonton wrappers, in a large bowl and mix until it is smooth and without lumps.

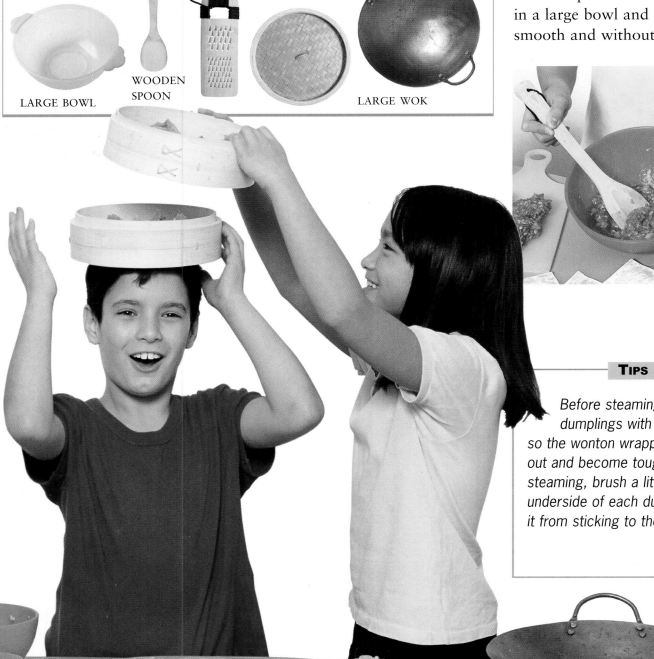

TIPS & TRICKS

Before steaming, cover the dumplings with a damp cloth so the wonton wrappers do not dry out and become tough. After steaming, brush a little oil on the underside of each dumpling to stop it from sticking to the plate.

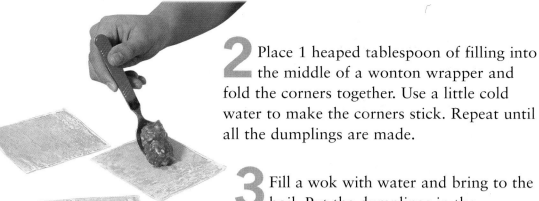

2 Place 1 heaped tablespoon of filling into the middle of a wonton wrapper and fold the corners together. Use a little cold water to make the corners stick. Repeat until all the dumplings are made.

3 Fill a wok with water and bring to the boil. Put the dumplings in the steamer and balance it on chopsticks in the wok. Cover the steamer with the lid.

4 Steam for about 20 minutes, or until the meat is cooked through. Serve the dim sum warm with some light soy sauce and sliced ginger or chilli sauce.

Ingredients

2 teaspoons grated fresh ginger

500 g (1 lb) finely ground (minced) pork

250 g (8 oz) chopped shelled shrimp

1 tablespoon light soy sauce

½ tablespoon sesame oil

1 teaspoon sugar

1 egg

2 tablespoons cornflour

pinch of white pepper

1 packet of wonton wrappers

Chinese Sweetcorn Soup with Crab Meat

Cold drinks are not normally served at a Chinese family meal. Instead, people usually have a bowl of hot soup. Soups have a long tradition in Chinese cuisine. In fact, a Chinese poem written over 2200 years ago talks about a person eating a "sour and bitter soup."

1 Place the chicken stock in a large pan and bring to the boil. Add the sweetcorn and sliced ginger and simmer over low heat for about 15 minutes, or until the corn is tender.

Ingredients

 1.5 litres (3 pints) chicken stock (made with hot water and a chicken stock cube)

 250 g (8 oz) sweetcorn

250 g (8 oz) cooked crab meat

 3–4 slices fresh ginger

 1 egg white

1 teaspoon sesame oil

1 tablespoon light soy sauce

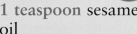 pinch of salt

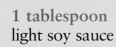 2 teaspoons cornflour

 pinch of white pepper

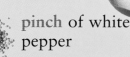 pinch of sugar

 2 spring onions, chopped

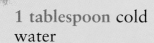 1 tablespoon cold water

2 While the sweetcorn is simmering, mix the cornflour, soy sauce, salt, pepper, sugar, and water in a small bowl until it becomes a smooth paste.

3 When the sweetcorn is cooked, pour the soy sauce paste into the soup. Turn the heat up to medium and stir until the soup starts to boil.

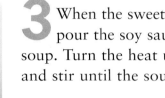

4 Use a spoon to add the crab meat to the soup. Stir gently so that you don't get splashed with the boiling soup. Simmer for 5 more minutes.

6 Use a slotted spoon to remove the slices of ginger from the soup. Sprinkle with spring onions and extra pepper. Serve hot.

5 In another bowl, beat the egg white and the sesame oil together. Now slowly add this mixture to the soup. As you pour the mixture into the pan, stir with a fork or a pair of chopsticks. The egg white should become thin and stringy.

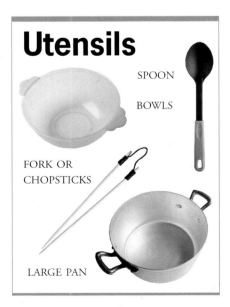

Utensils

SPOON

BOWLS

FORK OR CHOPSTICKS

LARGE PAN

Lentil Soup

This recipe for lentil soup is a special dish which is often served at celebrations of Islamic rites of passage, such as the coming of age when boys start to attend the mosque. It is a filling and nutritious dish that is fun and easy to make.

1 Place the black beans and chick peas in a large bowl. Pour over enough water to cover. Let soak overnight.

Utensils

LARGE SAUCEPAN

SLOTTED SPATULA

BOWLS

FRYING PAN

Ingredients

200 g (7 oz) dried lentils

200 g (7 oz) dried chick peas

200 g (7 oz) rice

1 teaspoon salt

1 small onion, finely chopped

½ teaspoon caraway seeds

4 tablespoons extra virgin olive oil

200 g (7 oz) dried black beans

1.5–2 litres (3–4 pints) water

2 Cook the rice in a large saucepan of water until tender.

3 Sauté the onions in the oil until lightly browned.

4 Drain the beans and place in a large saucepan with the lentils and water and cook for 1 hour, or until tender. Add the cooked rice to the pan.

5 Add the onions to the pan and simmer over low heat for 10 more minutes. Serve hot.

TIPS & TRICKS

Cooking the rice separately will speed up the thickening of the soup. Cook the rice in salted boiling water for about 15 minutes, or until tender.

27

Tortilla Soup

Sopa de tortilla is a classic Mexican soup. In Mexican cooking there are two types of soups. *Sopas secas*, or dry soups, have rice or noodles that soak up the broth (the liquid) while they are cooking. *Sopas aguadas*, or wet soups, are the more liquid soups that we usually eat. *Sopa de tortilla* is a wet soup made with chicken stock. To prepare this recipe, first make the chicken stock by adding a chicken stock cube to 500 ml (1 pint) of boiling water, stirring until it dissolves.

1 Chop the onion, garlic, celery, and courgette into small pieces.

TIPS & TRICKS

It is usually best to do all the cutting and chopping before you begin cooking. Then you will have everything ready when you need it. When chopping ingredients, try to cut them all about the same size. This allows them to cook at the same speed.

2 Warm a saucepan over medium heat. Once the pan is hot, add the oil and vegetables to it. Cook until they are soft.

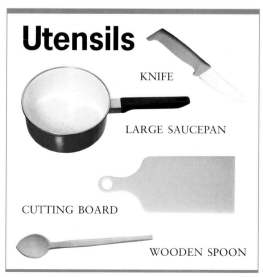

Utensils

KNIFE

LARGE SAUCEPAN

CUTTING BOARD

WOODEN SPOON

Ingredients

1 small onion

2 cloves garlic

1 stalk celery, chopped

2 small courgettes

2 tablespoons vegetable oil

1 tin tomatoes 400 g (14 oz) OR

500 g (1 lb) crushed tomatoes

250 ml (½ pint) water

500 ml (1 pint) chicken stock

250 g (8 oz) sweetcorn

½ teaspoon cumin

tortilla chips

1 avocado, peeled

3 Add all the other ingredients, except the avocado and tortilla chips. Simmer over low heat for 30 minutes, stirring often.

4 When you are ready to serve, slice the avocado. Ladle the soup into serving bowls. Add some avocado and tortilla chips to each bowl, and serve.

Mexican Beef and Potato Soup

This healthy soup is called *caldito* in Spanish. Mexicans say it tastes *"Mejon en la manana!"* or "Better the next day!" This is an ideal dish if you are planning to invite friends for a Mexican meal and have a number of recipes to prepare. Make *caldito* the day before and just reheat it before serving. *Caldito* is a hearty soup and is perfect for winter evenings. As an extra touch, try adding some chopped spring onions just before serving.

Utensils

KNIFE

FRYING PAN

CUTTING BOARD

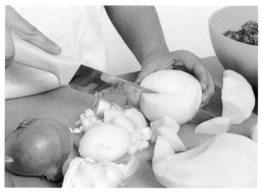

1 Chop the onion and fresh chillies (if you are using them instead of tinned chillies). Mince the garlic and dice the potatoes.

2 Place the beef, onion, potatoes, and garlic in a large frying pan over a medium heat. Stir and cook until the meat is browned. Make sure there is no pink left in the meat.

4 Add the water or chicken stock and stir well.

5 Add the green chillies and stir. Simmer over low heat for 30 minutes.

3 Drain any liquid that has formed in the pan. Ask an adult to help you. Remember the pan will be heavy and hot! Stir fry until the potatoes start to soften.

31

Ingredients

1 small red onion, chopped

2 cloves garlic, minced

5 medium potatoes, diced

1 lb (500 g) minced beef

2 small tins chopped green chillies or 8 to 10 fresh chillies, roasted, peeled, veined, and deseeded

750 ml (1½ pints) water or chicken stock

TIPS & TRICKS

When in the kitchen, make sure you are not wearing long, loose sleeves that may get caught on a handle. Wear an apron to protect your clothes. Wash your hands thoroughly after cutting chillies as it is painful if you get chilli juice in your eyes.

6 The next day, reheat and serve hot with tortillas.

Classic Pizza

Even if you have a great pizza place in your neighbourhood, try making your own at home. Making pizza is simple and fun. Two main things to remember are kneading the dough properly and leaving it long enough to rise. This recipe is for the classic Margherita pizza, which was invented in Naples, Italy, for Queen Margherita of Savoy, in June 1889. You can vary it by adding ham or mushrooms, or some of your other favourite toppings.

1 In a bowl, dissolve the yeast in 125 ml (¼ pint) of warm water, mixing well. Set the yeast aside for 15 minutes. Sift the flour and salt into another large bowl.

2 Gradually work the yeast mixture into the flour. Flour your hands and use your knuckles and fists to work the dough until it is smooth and elastic.

3 Form the dough into a ball, and wrap it loosely in a clean cotton cloth. Leave it in the bowl in a warm sheltered place to rise or cover the bowl with a cloth for at least 30 minutes. Preheat the oven to 230°C/450°F/gas 7.

4 Grease a rectangular or circular pizza pan and use your fingertips to gently stretch the dough out to cover the bottom.

5 Open the tin of crushed tomatoes and spread them over the dough. If using whole tomatoes, put them in a bowl and squash them with your fingers first. Chop or grate the mozzarella cheese and spread it on top of the tomatoes.

6 Sprinkle with the salt, basil, and oregano. Drizzle with the oil and bake in the oven for about 20 minutes.

Ingredients

500 g (1 lb) plain flour

1 teaspoon salt

20 g (⅔ oz) compressed baker's yeast or 1 packet active dry yeast

1 tin (400 g/14 oz) crushed tomatoes

150 g (5 oz) mozzarella cheese

1 tablespoon extra virgin olive oil

pinch of fresh or dried oregano and basil

Utensils

LARGE BOWL

PIZZA TRAY

TIPS & TRICKS

Ask an adult to open the tin of tomatoes and also to take the pizza out of the oven. If you do handle the hot pizza tray yourself, be sure to use thick oven gloves to protect your hands.

Quiche Lorraine

A quiche is a savoury pie or tart. There are many different types of quiche, but Quiche Lorraine is the classic one. It was invented by a French cook in the northern French city of Nancy in the 16th century. The French serve quiche as a first course, but it is so filling and nourishing that it can be served as a meal in itself.

Ingredients

450 g (15 oz) plain flour

180 g (6 oz) butter

pinch of salt

1 kg (2 lb) dried beans

90 ml (⅙ pint) ice cold water

125 g (4 oz) bacon, in thin slices

125 g (4 oz) emmental cheese, diced

3 eggs

375 ml (⅔ pint) fresh cream

pinch of freshly grated nutmeg

1 Sift the flour and salt into a mixing bowl. Add the chopped butter and work it in using your fingers until the mixture is the consistency of breadcrumbs. Gradually pour in the water and mix until the dough is smooth and elastic. Shape it into a ball, wrap in plastic wrap, and refrigerate for 30 minutes.

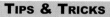
TIPS & TRICKS

This quiche is also good if made with ham instead of bacon. Ask an adult to help when putting dishes in or taking them out of the oven, or remember to use oven gloves.

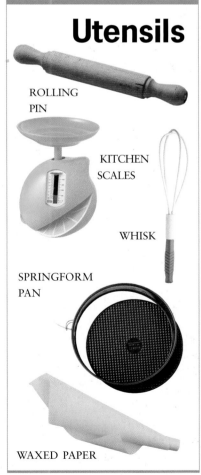

2 Preheat the oven to 180°C/350°F/gas 4. Roll the dough out on a floured work surface to about 5 mm (¼ inch) thick.

3 Use the dough to line a buttered and floured 26 cm (10 inch) diameter springform pan.

4 Prick the dough on the bottom of the pan with a fork. Cover with a sheet of waxed paper and fill with the dried beans. Bake for 20 minutes. Discard the paper and beans.

Utensils

ROLLING PIN

KITCHEN SCALES

WHISK

SPRINGFORM PAN

5 Brown the bacon lightly in a frying pan and place on the baked pastry shell. Sprinkle with the cheese.

WAXED PAPER

6 Beat the eggs and cream with a whisk. Add a pinch of salt and nutmeg. Pour the mixture over the bacon and cheese. Bake for 30 minutes or until set and pale gold.

Pasta with Tomato and Basil Sauce

Pasta is the national dish in Italy, where it is served every day. Tomato sauce is one of the most popular sauces for pasta. Tomatoes were introduced to Italy from Mexico and Central America by Spanish explorers during the 16th century. Serve the dish with style by saying *"Buon appetito!"* which means "Enjoy!"

1 tin (400 g/ 14 oz) tomatoes

OR

500 g (1 lb) fresh tomatoes

6 fresh basil leaves, torn into pieces

2 cloves garlic, minced

500 g (1 lb) penne pasta

4 tablespoons extra virgin olive oil

4 tablespoons grated parmesan cheese

pinch of table salt for the sauce and 2 tablespoons coarse salt to cook the pasta

If you have some extra sauce left over, spoon it over a slice of toasted bread for a tasty snack.

1 Place a large pan of cold water on the stove over high heat. Drain the liquid from the tinned tomatoes, place them in a medium pan, and mash. If fresh tomatoes are used, peel them with a potato peeler or knife, chop them into cubes, and place in a medium pan.

2 Add the oil, garlic, and salt to the tomatoes. Place the pan over medium heat and partially cover. Cook for about 30 minutes, stirring often to prevent sticking. With an adult's help remove from the heat and add the basil.

3 When the water in the large pan is boiling, add the coarse salt and then the penne. Cook for the amount of time shown on the package, stirring often. Drain the pasta in the colander and transfer it to a serving dish.

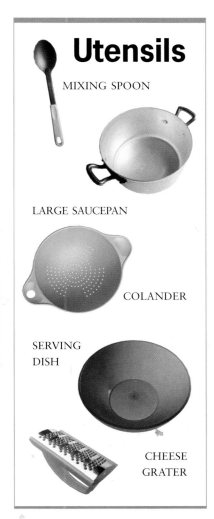

Utensils

MIXING SPOON

LARGE SAUCEPAN

COLANDER

SERVING DISH

CHEESE GRATER

4 Spoon the tomato sauce over the cooked pasta and mix well. Grate the parmesan cheese over the top. If the cheese is already grated, sprinkle over the pasta. Serve immediately.

This sauce is good with all pasta shapes, including spaghetti, macaroni, and rotini. Be sure to try it with wholewheat or spinach pasta too!

TIPS & TRICKS

Be very careful when draining the pasta. The large pot of boiling water and pasta will be very heavy. Ask an adult to help you lift it. The trick with pasta is getting the cooking time right. It should be soft but still firm when you chew it. Do not cook it so much that it gets mushy and tasteless!

Fresh Pasta with Tomato Sauce

Tagliatelle is a fresh noodle pasta that comes from Emilia-Romagna in central Italy. It should be 8 mm (⅓ inch) wide. If it is wider than this, it is known as *pappardelle* and if it is thinner, it is called *tagliolini*. The sauce recipe is also from Emilia-Romagna. It features delicious Parma ham, called *prosciutto,* which is a speciality from the city of Parma in that region.

1 Put the *prosciutto* on a cutting board. Cut it first into strips and then into cubes. Hold the knife firmly in one hand and keep your fingers well away from the blade.

Ingredients

500 g (1 lb) fresh *tagliatelle* pasta

150 g (5 oz) *prosciutto* (Parma ham)

6–8 fresh tomatoes or 500 g (1 lb) tinned tomatoes

125 g (4 oz) butter

pinch of table salt for the sauce and 2 tablespoons coarse salt to cook the pasta

6 tablespoons grated parmesan cheese

TIPS & TRICKS

Always turn the handle of pots and pans on the stove inward so that you do not bump them. Place the large pan of boiling water for the pasta on a back burner where it is safer.

2 Use a potato peeler or knife to peel the tomatoes, then chop them coarsely, or open a can of tomatoes and squash them in a bowl using a fork. Place the tomatoes in a medium saucepan together with the *prosciutto* and the butter.

3 Mix well and cook over medium heat for about 30 minutes. Stir occasionally with a wooden spoon. Add salt to taste. Place a large pan of cold water on the stove over high heat.

4 When the water is boiling in the large pan, add the coarse salt followed by the *tagliatelle*. Cook until *al dente*, or just tender.

LADLE

CHEESE GRATER

KNIFE

CUTTING BOARD

SAUCEPAN

WOODEN SPOON

5 Drain the pasta in a colander. Transfer it to a large serving dish. Ladle the tomato sauce over the top and sprinkle with the parmesan. Toss well and serve hot.

Pasta with Basil Sauce

This pasta sauce is quick and easy to make. You just have to mix the ingredients in a food processor, cook the pasta, combine the two, and serve! Basil sauce, called pesto in Italian, comes from the city of Genoa, on the Italian Riviera. Located between the mountains and the Mediterranean Sea, Genoa has a mild climate where herbs such as basil grow well.

Utensils

MIXING SPOON

HAND HELD
FOOD PROCESSOR

CHEESE
GRATER

COLANDER

1 Place a large pan of cold water on the stove over high heat. Separate the basil leaves from the stems. Place the leaves in a colander and rinse. Drain well and dry on a clean cloth.

2 Grate the cheeses. If you have one, use a grater with a little catcher underneath so that it is easier to gather up the grated cheese.

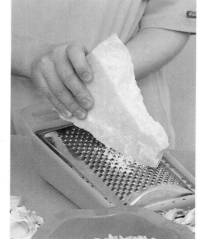

Ingredients

2 tablespoons
toasted pine nuts

40 fresh basil
leaves

350 g (12 oz)
linguine pasta

pinch of table salt for
the sauce and 2 tablespoons
coarse salt to cook the pasta

150 ml (¹/₄ pint)
extra virgin olive oil

1–2 cloves
garlic

2 tablespoons
each parmesan and
pecorino cheese

3 Place the basil, cheeses, pine nuts, garlic, oil, and salt in a bowl and chop with a hand held processor. If you have a food processor, place the ingredients in the bowl and chop until the sauce is creamy. If the sauce is too thick, add 1–2 tablespoons of boiling water from the pan.

4 When the water in the large pot is boiling, add the coarse salt and then the pasta. Cook for the amount of time shown on the packet. Drain the pasta in a colander and transfer it to a serving dish. Pour the basil sauce over the top and toss well. Serve immediately.

TIPS & TRICKS

When using the food processor make sure your hands are completely dry. Never put your fingers inside the processor or near the blade of a hand held processor. To scrape the mixture off the sides of the processor, turn it off and use a spatula. Ask an adult to help you.

Baked Macaroni

To make this dish you will need to prepare a Béchamel sauce. Béchamel is a basic and well known French white sauce. It was invented by Louis de Béchamel, who was head butler at the grand court of King Louis XIV in the 17th century. Béchamel goes particularly well with pasta, but is also delicious with vegetables baked in the oven.

Utensils

CHEESE GRATER

WOODEN SPOON

COLANDER

SAUCEPAN

OVENPROOF BAKING DISH

1 Melt the butter in a saucepan over low heat. Remove from the heat and sift in the flour, stirring continuously so that no lumps form.

2 Return to the heat and cook for 1–2 minutes, so that the flour is lightly "toasted."

3 Pour in the milk a little at a time, stirring continuously. Add salt, pepper, and nutmeg to taste. After a few minutes, the mixture will boil. Cook for 3–4 minutes, stirring continuously.

4 Preheat the oven to 200°C/400°F/gas 6. Lightly butter an ovenproof dish and cover the bottom with a layer of cooked pasta. Curl the long strands around to cover the dish as evenly as you can. You can also use other types of short or long pasta.

5 Cover the pasta with a layer of Béchamel, followed by a layer of gruyère and a sprinkling of parmesan. Repeat until all the ingredients are used up.

Ingredients

4 tablespoons butter

4 tablespoons plain flour

salt and black pepper to taste

pinch of freshly grated nutmeg

500 ml (1 pint) warm milk

300 g (10 oz) precooked ziti pasta

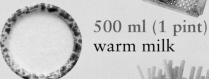

150 g (5 oz) gruyère cheese, grated

125 g (4 oz) parmesan cheese, grated

TIPS & TRICKS

To cook the pasta, place a large pot of lightly salted cold water over high heat. When it is boiling, add the pasta and cook for the time indicated on the packet. When the pasta is cooked, ask an adult to help you drain it in the colander.

6 Bake for about 20 minutes, or until a golden crust, or "gratin" has formed. Ask an adult to remove the hot dish from the oven and serve immediately.

Long-Life Noodles

Noodles are popular in Chinese cuisine. They are always served at birthday parties, because the long strands are believed to be symbols of long life. To have a long life, people try to eat the noodles whole, without biting through the strands. Eating noodles whole takes quite a bit of practice, so make this dish often!

2 Heat the oil in a wok. When it is hot, stir fry the minced ginger and garlic until golden.

Utensils

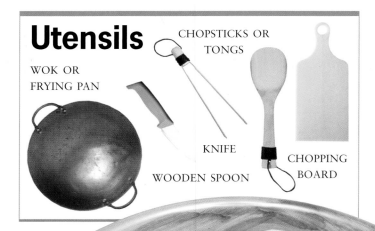

CHOPSTICKS OR TONGS

WOK OR FRYING PAN

KNIFE

WOODEN SPOON

CHOPPING BOARD

1 If using dried noodles, follow the instructions on the packet to cook them. Drain and set aside.

3 Add the pork and stir fry until it is well cooked and golden.

TIPS & TRICKS

To prevent the cooked noodles from sticking together, toss them in a little oil. Then lay them on a plate until you need them. Stir the noodles with care after adding them to the wok to avoid breaking them. If you cannot find fish cake in an Asian supermarket, use cooked shrimps instead. If you cannot find fresh bean sprouts, thinly sliced Chinese cabbage works well. Both vegetables give a crunch to the dish and balance out the soft noodles.

44

Ingredients

250 g (8 oz) fresh or dried egg noodles

2 tablespoons vegetable oil

1 teaspoon fresh ginger, minced

2–3 cloves garlic, minced

125 g (4 oz) bean sprouts

125 g (4 oz) sliced pork

90 g (3 oz) Chinese fish cake

1 tablespoon light soy sauce

1 tablespoon oyster sauce

4 Add the bean sprouts and Chinese fish cake and stir fry for 2–3 minutes more.

5 Add the noodles to the wok and stir fry for 2–3 minutes more.

6 Pour in the soy sauce and oyster sauce, and stir fry until all the ingredients are well mixed. Serve hot.

Potato Dumplings with Meat Sauce

These little potato dumplings are a favourite dish all over Italy. The "gn" in *gnocchi* has the same pronunciation as the word "gnome," while the "ch" is pronounced like a "k." *Gnocchi* originally came from Verona, in northern Italy, where they were served with melted butter, sugar, and cinnamon. In Tuscany, they are called *topini*, which means "little mice."

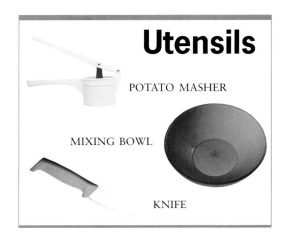

Utensils

POTATO MASHER

MIXING BOWL

KNIFE

1 Cook the unpeeled potatoes in a large pot of boiling water. Drain and set aside. When cool, remove the skins using your fingers, then mash.

2 Dust your hands with flour and begin working the flour and salt into the potatoes. Continue until the mixture is smooth and well mixed but still soft.

Ingredients

1 kg (2 lb) boiling potatoes

450 g (15 oz) plain flour

pinch of salt

400 g (14 oz) jar of ready-made Italian meat sauce

4 tablespoons grated parmesan cheese

3 Take a handful of the mixture and roll it out into a long, thin "sausage" on a floured work surface. Cut the sausage into lengths about 2–3 cm (1 inch) long. Place a big pot full of cold water on the stove over a high heat.

4 Pick up each dumpling in one hand and run the prongs of a fork along the edges so that it has lines running around it. If this is too difficult or takes too long, leave this step out. The *gnocchi* will still taste great!

5 Place the *gnocchi* on a lightly floured cloth. When the water is boiling, add a first batch of about 30 *gnocchi*. When they float up to the top, they are cooked. Scoop them out with a slotted spoon, and transfer to a serving dish. Repeat until all the *gnocchi* are cooked. Heat the meat sauce and pour over the *gnocchi*. Sprinkle with the parmesan and serve.

TIPS & TRICKS

To avoid being splashed by boiling water, place the gnocchi on a small, lightly floured dish, dip the edge into the water, and let them slip gently into the pot.

Parmesan and Saffron Risotto

Rice was introduced to Western Europe by Arabs during the Middle Ages. Risotto was invented in the northern Italian city of Milan, where it is still a classic rice dish. This is a very good way to prepare rice because it cooks slowly, absorbing the flavours of all the other ingredients. Saffron adds a touch of colour, turning the rice red or gold, depending on how much you add.

Ingredients

1 medium red onion

6 tablespoons butter

400 g (14 oz) rice (preferably Italian Arborio rice)

Italians traditionally cook risotto with wine. If preferred, use chicken stock

1 litre (2 pints) chicken stock, made with boiling water and 1 stock cube

1 packet saffron

6 tablespoons grated parmesan cheese

1 Chop the onion coarsely using a half-moon chopper or knife. In a deep-bottomed saucepan, sauté the onion in half the butter until it is golden.

TIPS & TRICKS

Keep the saucepan with the hot stock on the stove next to the risotto. This will keep it warm and make it easier and safer for you to add as the rice cooks.

2 Add the rice to the saucepan and stir continuously over medium heat for about 2 minutes. Hold the saucepan firmly by the handle while stirring. The rice should swell and be lightly toasted.

3 Dissolve the chicken stock cube in the hot water. Begin adding the stock to the rice a ladleful at a time, stirring as it is absorbed by the rice. Repeat until all of the stock has been absorbed.

Utensils

HALF-MOON CHOPPER

LADLE

CHEESE GRATER

CUTTING BOARD

WOODEN SPOON

DEEP-BOTTOMED SAUCEPAN

4 Continue cooking and gradually adding more stock for 15–20 minutes. Stir all the time so that the rice does not stick to the pan. Taste the rice after about 15 minutes to see if it is cooked. It should be soft, but firm or *"al dente,"* which means "firm to the bite."

5 When the rice is cooked, remove it from the heat and stir in the remaining butter.

6 Add the saffron and stir well so that the rice is evenly coloured. Finally, stir in the parmesan and serve.

Fried Rice

This dish is very popular in Chinese restaurants. Usually fried rice is served in Chinese homes as a one-dish meal, although it is also used instead of steamed rice to go with a meal. At special banquets, fried rice is served towards the end of the meal to fill up anyone who did not get enough to eat!

WOODEN SPOON OR SPATULA

CHOPSTICKS OR FORK

WOK OR LARGE FRYING PAN

Ingredients

250 g (8 oz) chopped ham, or cooked shrimps

1 egg

250 g (8 oz) fresh or thawed frozen vegetables

1 kg (2 lb) cooked long-grain rice

2 cloves garlic, minced

1 tablespoon light soy sauce

2 tablespoons vegetable oil

1 Add 1 tablespoon of the oil to the wok then place over a medium heat.

2 Add the garlic and stir fry until it turns a pale golden brown. Be careful not to burn the garlic because it will make the dish taste bitter.

3 Add the ham or shrimps, together with the vegetables. Stir fry for 1 minute.

4 Add the rice and stir fry until all the ingredients are well mixed. Place the rice mixture on a plate. Add the remaining oil to the wok.

5 Beat the egg in a bowl, then add it to the wok. Stir with a fork or chopsticks to scramble the egg. When cooked, put the rice mixture back into the wok. Pour the soy sauce on top and stir fry until well mixed. Serve hot.

TIPS & TRICKS

Fried rice should not be sticky – the grains should be separate and "dry." To get dry rice, use rice left over from the day before. If you do not have any rice leftovers, make sure that the rice you use is cooked and then left to cool before you start preparing your fried rice.

Mexican Rice

Rice was introduced to Mexico by the Spanish. It has become very popular and is used in starters, main courses, and desserts. This rice and vegetable recipe is tasty enough to be served on its own for dinner. If you like hot and spicy food, try serving this with the Hot Mexican Salsa recipe on pages 8–9.

1 Chop the onion, tomato, and pepper. Set aside until later.

2 Place a frying pan on the stove at a medium heat. Add the oil to the pan and warm it up. Add the rice and stir until it is light brown.

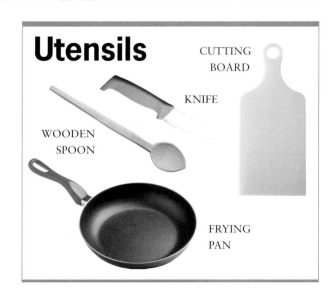

Utensils

CUTTING BOARD

KNIFE

WOODEN SPOON

FRYING PAN

3 Add the vegetables and stir until they are tender but not mushy.

4 Dissolve the stock cube in the water and stir into the vegetables. When the water begins to simmer, cover with a lid. Cook for 12–15 minutes, or until the rice is cooked. Serve hot.

53

TIPS & TRICKS

Use a long-handled wooden spoon to stir the rice. It will keep the heat away from your hand, and it will not damage the surface of your frying pan. While stirring, make sure that you scrape every part of the bottom of the pan. Occasionally scrape the sides of the pan to make sure everything is mixed together.

Ingredients

1 onion

2 tomatoes

1 green pepper

1 tablespoon vegetable oil

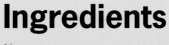
500 g (1 lb) long-grain rice

500 ml (1 pint) water

1 vegetable or chicken stock cube

Cheese Crêpes

Crêpes are one of the most famous French dishes, so to be a true French chef you must learn how to make them. Luckily, they are not very difficult. Crêpes can be served with savoury fillings, such as cheese and ham, or with sweet ones, such as sugar, jam, chocolate, and whipped cream. Even today, there are crêpe stalls on many street corners in Paris and other cities in France.

54

TIPS & TRICKS

Each time you add batter to the frying pan, add a little more melted butter first. Hold the frying pan firmly by the handle as you cook the crêpes. If you do not have gruyère cheese, use a thin slice of cheddar, or any other kind that melts well, in its place.

Utensils

FRYING PAN

MIXING BOWL

EGG BEATER

WHISK

SLOTTED SPATULA

Ingredients

225 g (7½ oz) plain flour

pinch of salt

250 ml (½ pint) milk

2 eggs

2 tablespoons butter + extra to cook

8 thin slices gruyère or other cheese

8 thin slices ham

6 Return the folded crêpes to the pan long enough to melt the cheese. Serve them warm.

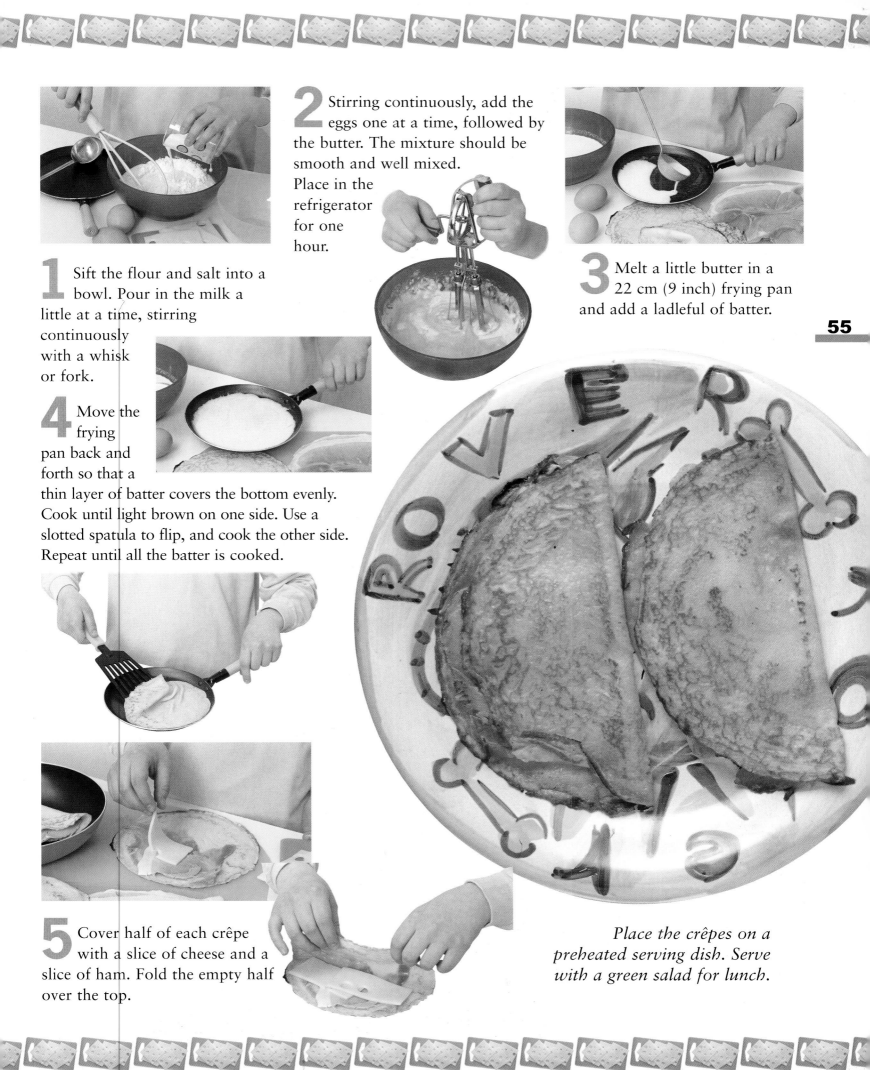

2 Stirring continuously, add the eggs one at a time, followed by the butter. The mixture should be smooth and well mixed. Place in the refrigerator for one hour.

1 Sift the flour and salt into a bowl. Pour in the milk a little at a time, stirring continuously with a whisk or fork.

3 Melt a little butter in a 22 cm (9 inch) frying pan and add a ladleful of batter.

4 Move the frying pan back and forth so that a thin layer of batter covers the bottom evenly. Cook until light brown on one side. Use a slotted spatula to flip, and cook the other side. Repeat until all the batter is cooked.

5 Cover half of each crêpe with a slice of cheese and a slice of ham. Fold the empty half over the top.

Place the crêpes on a preheated serving dish. Serve with a green salad for lunch.

Tomato Omelet

Omelets are quick and easy to make. They are also nutritious and fun to serve. They can be eaten plain, with herbs, or filled with cheese, tomatoes, ham or any of your favourite ingredients. Omelets are also practical when unexpected friends drop by. If eggs are the only food you have in your fridge, you can offer them this delicious treat.

Ingredients

1 onion

4 ripe tomatoes

2 tablespoons extra virgin olive oil

salt and black pepper to taste

6 eggs

1 bunch parsley

1 On a chopping board, slice the onion thinly with a sharp knife. Hold the knife firmly by the handle, and keep your fingers well away from the blade. Ask an adult to help.

TIPS & TRICKS

While cooking the omelet, make sure that the handle of the frying pan does not stick out. You might knock it onto yourself, or the floor, as you pass by.

2 Place a pan of water over high heat. When the water boils, turn off the heat and carefully add the tomatoes. Leave for 2 minutes, then remove with a slotted spoon. When the tomatoes have cooled down, remove the skins with your fingers. Chop the tomatoes into tiny pieces.

3 Heat the oil in a frying pan. Add the onion and tomato, season with salt and pepper, and cook over a medium-low heat for 15 minutes. Hold the handle of the pan while you stir it with a wooden spoon.

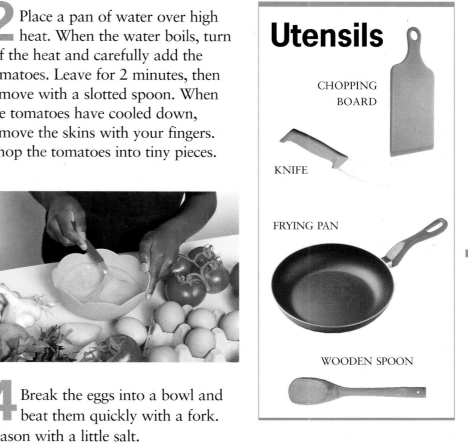

4 Break the eggs into a bowl and beat them quickly with a fork. Season with a little salt.

5 Lightly oil another frying pan and place over medium-low heat. Pour in half the eggs and cook for 4–5 minutes. Move the pan gently from side to side as the omelet cooks. Remove the omelet from the heat and slide it onto a serving dish.

6 Cook the second omelet as shown above. Pour half the tomato sauce onto one half of each omelet, sprinkle with chopped parsley and use a wooden spoon to fold them in two. Serve and enjoy!

Singapore Omelet

Traditionally, eggs are not served as a main dish in Chinese cooking. This style of omelet, however, has become popular. It is quick and easy to prepare, and can be served at breakfast, lunch, or dinner. Try adding your favourite foods to it.

Utensils

CHOPSTICKS

BOWL

SLOTTED SPATULA

FRYING PAN

1 Combine the onion, meat, soy sauce, and salt in a mixing bowl. Mix until it is smooth and without large lumps.

2 Beat the eggs in a separate bowl until they are light and frothy. Add the egg to the ham and onion mixture.

Ingredients

1 small white onion, chopped

250 g (8 oz) diced ham

1 handful bean sprouts

½ tablespoon light soy sauce

2 eggs

1 teaspoon salt

2 spring onions, chopped

2 tablespoons vegetable oil

For the sauce

125 ml (¼ pint) chicken stock

2 teaspoons thick soy sauce

pinch of sugar

2 teaspoons cornflour

---

3 Heat the oil in a frying pan and slowly pour in all of the egg mixture. When the omelet gets a little puffy and the underside is golden brown, add the bean sprouts and spring onions. Flip the omelet over and cook until the other side is brown too.

59

4 While the omelet cooks, mix all the ingredients for the sauce together in a saucepan and bring to a boil. Pour the sauce over the omelet or serve separately.

TIPS & TRICKS

Try using crab meat or diced roast pork instead of the ham in this recipe. When cooking the omelet, let the sides set and then push them towards the centre of the pan. Tip the pan and let the excess egg mixture flow to the sides. Your omelet will cook more evenly and it will be easier to turn over. Also shake the pan while cooking to make the omelet fluffier.

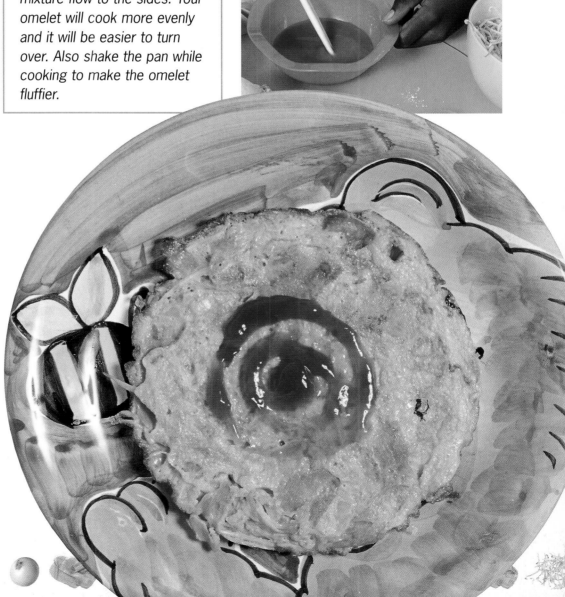

Meatballs with Tomato Sauce

These meatballs are bound to become one of your favourite dishes. The bread swells during cooking, making them soft as well as tasty. You can cut them with a fork and finish them in no time! The mixture is also fun to make because you can do it all with your hands. Who could resist squeezing the soft mince together with the other ingredients and rolling it into balls?

2 Grate the cheese and bread together into a large bowl. Keep your fingertips away from the grater.

1 Combine the tomatoes, salt, and oil in a deep saucepan. Cook over low heat for about 15 minutes, stirring often.

Utensils

GRATER

DEEP
FRYING
PAN

3 Combine the meat with the bread, cheese, eggs, salt, and pepper in a large mixing bowl. Mix well with your hands. Add a ladleful of the tomato sauce and stir it in with a spoon. Let the mixture cool.

4 Rinse your hands in cold water to stop the mixture from sticking to them. Use your hands to form the mixture into smooth round balls each about the size of a large plum. Repeat this step until you have used up all the mixture. Place the meatballs on a plate.

5 Add the meatballs carefully to the tomato sauce, one at a time. Cook them in the sauce over low heat for 20–30 minutes without stirring. Shake the pan very gently from time to time. Serve the meatballs with the sauce spooned over the top of them.

Ingredients

1.5 litres (3 pints) tomato purée, not concentrated

salt to taste

4 tablespoons extra virgin olive oil

500 g (1 lb) lean minced beef

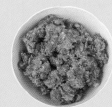

1 loaf crusty white bread

3 eggs

125 g (4 oz) parmesan cheese, grated

black pepper to taste

TIPS & TRICKS

Add the meatballs to the sauce very gently so that they do not break up. A good way to do this is to dip a tablespoon into cold water and scoop up a meatball. Dip it into the sauce, then pull the spoon out from under it.

Chicken with Rice

This dish will warm you up on cold winter evenings, although it takes a while to cook. Keep an eye on the pan to make sure it does not burn or boil over. Try experimenting with the flavour – use small amounts of garlic, ginger, or lemon juice.

1 Simmer the chicken breasts in a pan of boiling water for about 15 minutes. Remove the breasts, and save the water in the pot. This water is now chicken stock.

2 Rinse the rice under cold running water. Place 1 litre (2 pints) of the chicken stock in a pan and add the rice and ginger. Bring the pan to the boil, then lower the heat. Simmer without a lid for about 1½ hours, or until the rice is very soft. Keep the heat low so that it does not boil over, and stir often so the rice does not stick. If it becomes too thick to stir, add more chicken stock to the pan.

3 While the rice is cooking, chop the cooked chicken breasts and place to one side.

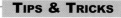

TIPS & TRICKS

For a different flavour, replace the chicken with the same quantity of sliced fish or prawns. Also try using half long grain rice and half glutinous rice, so that the dish is thicker and creamier. Some Chinese grocery stores also sell something called "broken rice." This rice cooks more quickly and it is perfect for this recipe.

Ingredients

2 chicken breasts, boneless and skinless

250 g (8 oz) long-grain rice

4 slices fresh ginger

salt to taste

few drops of sesame oil

few drops of light soy sauce

1 tablespoon chopped coriander

2 spring onions, chopped

Utensils

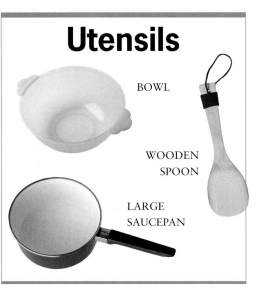

BOWL

WOODEN SPOON

LARGE SAUCEPAN

4 When it is ready, the mixture should be thick and creamy.

5 Place the rice in a serving bowl. Drizzle it with sesame oil and soy sauce and stir. Top with the chicken and season with salt. Garnish with coriander and spring onions.

Chicken Skewers

Skewers are a common dish in many countries of the Mediterranean. This recipe comes from southern France and the island of Corsica. Skewers are fun to make because you can alternate the meat and other ingredients on the skewers to make each one look different. When cooked, you can slide the ingredients off the skewer with a fork. The grapefruit in this recipe can be replaced with cherry tomatoes or another vegetable.

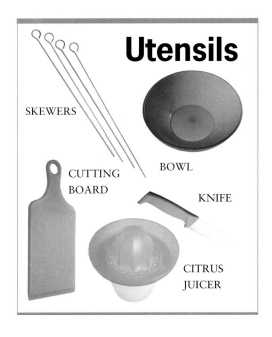

Utensils

SKEWERS

BOWL

CUTTING BOARD

KNIFE

CITRUS JUICER

1 Place the chicken breasts and pancetta or bacon on a chopping board. Chop them into bite-sized pieces.

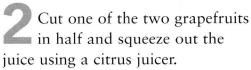

2 Cut one of the two grapefruits in half and squeeze out the juice using a citrus juicer.

3 Beat the grapefruit juice with the oil and a little salt and pepper in a bowl. Add the chopped meat and mix well. Set aside to marinate for at least 30 minutes. Two hours is even better, if you have the time.

Ingredients

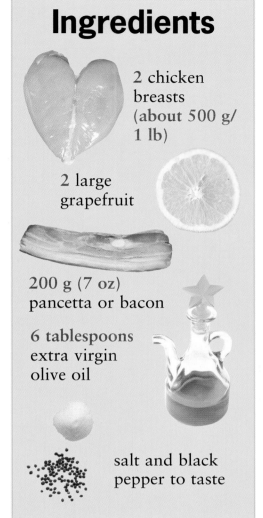

2 chicken breasts (about 500 g/ 1 lb)

2 large grapefruit

200 g (7 oz) pancetta or bacon

6 tablespoons extra virgin olive oil

salt and black pepper to taste

4 Peel the remaining grapefruit, removing as much of the inner skin as possible. Ask an adult to help you use a pointed knife to remove the remaining membrane, or skin covering each wedge.

TIPS & TRICKS

If using wooden skewers, soak them well in cold water first so they do not burn. These skewers can also be cooked over a barbecue or under the grill in the oven.

5 Stick a piece of chicken onto a skewer, then follow with a piece of pancetta, and then a piece of grapefruit. Repeat until the skewer is full. When all the skewers are ready, place them in a lightly oiled, nonstick frying pan over medium–high heat for about 15 minutes. Turn them often during cooking and sprinkle with a little salt. Ask an adult to help you.

Meat and Potato Pie

The combination of meat and potato purée is so good that this may become one of your favourite French foods. Potatoes were not always so well liked in France. When Monsieur Parmentier, who invented the dish, began growing potatoes in about 1785, no one liked them. Parmentier had to use tricks just to get people to taste them!

Ingredients

1 kg (2 lb) potatoes boiled in their skins

500 ml (1 pint) milk

6 tablespoons butter

300 g (10 oz) cooked meat, or uncooked mince

1 large onion

bunch of parsley

salt to taste

pinch of freshly grated nutmeg

1 When the potatoes have cooled after cooking, peel the skins with your fingers. Put the potatoes in a bowl. Preheat the oven to 200°C/400°F/gas 6.

5 Grease the ovenproof dish with a little butter and cover with a layer of potato. Add the meat. Cover with the remaining potato and top with the butter.

6 Bake for 20 minutes, or until golden brown on top.

2 Mash the potatoes with a potato masher. Add half the butter and stir with a whisk or wooden spoon. Gradually add the milk to make a smooth, creamy mixture. Season with salt, pepper, and nutmeg.

3 If using a piece of cooked meat, chop with a half-moon chopper or in a food processor until well ground. Chop the onion and cut the parsley into fine pieces.

4 Melt half the remaining butter in a frying pan and fry the onion and parsley. Add the meat and season with salt and pepper. Cook for 5 minutes over medium heat. Ask an adult to help you when using the stove.

Utensils

POTATO PEELER

HALF-MOON CHOPPER

WHISK

MIXING SPOON

FRYING PAN

OVENPROOF BAKING DISH

Wiener Schnitzel

Wiener schnitzel (Viennese cutlets), or beef escalopes, are named after Vienna, the capital city of Austria. Many people think the dish was invented there but food historians in Italy have found letters that prove it was actually invented in Milan, over 1000 years ago! These beef escalopes are tasty and quick to make. You can serve them with French fries and a green salad for a complete family meal.

1 Break the eggs into a small bowl, add a pinch of salt, and beat for 2–3 minutes with a fork.

2 Dry the beef escalopes with paper towels. Then sprinkle lightly with salt on both sides.

Ingredients

2 eggs

pinch of salt

2–4 beef escalopes

150 g (5 oz) dry bread-crumbs

250 ml (½ pint) olive oil for frying

3 Dip the beef escalopes one at a time into the bowl of egg. Make sure that every part of the meat is coated with egg. Let the extra egg drip back into the bowl as you lift the meat out.

4 Spread the bread crumbs out on a large plate. Lay each escalope in the bread crumbs and press down. Turn over and repeat. Shake off any extra bread crumbs.

Utensils

SLOTTED SPATULA

FRYING PAN

5 Heat the oil in a large frying pan and add the escalopes one or two at a time. Make sure they do not overlap. Cook until a deep golden crust forms. Then turn over to cook the other side. Remove from the pan and drain on paper towels. Serve hot.

Tofu with Pork

Tofu, also called bean curd, has a slightly nutty taste that blends in well with strong flavours. Tofu is made from soya milk and is very good for you. It is a common high-protein food in many parts of Asia where less meat is eaten than in America, Europe, and Australia. You can find tofu in Asian supermarkets and health food stores.

70

1 Place the oil, garlic, and ginger in a wok on a medium heat. Sauté for 2 minutes. Add all the other ingredients except the pork, tofu, and onions, and bring them to the boil.

TIPS & TRICKS

The sauce that is made in step 1 can be prepared in advance and stored in the refrigerator until you need it. If you do not like pork, use chicken or beef instead.

2 When the sauce is bubbling, add the pork and cook for about 10 minutes, stirring constantly.

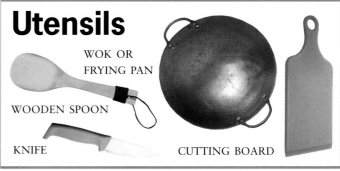

Utensils

WOK OR FRYING PAN

WOODEN SPOON

KNIFE

CUTTING BOARD

3 Cut the tofu into bite-sized pieces and slice the spring onions roughly. Take care to hold the knife firmly by the handle with one hand and hold the tofu and onions with your other hand. Keep your fingers well away from the blade at all times.

4 Add the tofu to the wok and stir carefully.

5 Sprinkle with the spring onions, and toss very carefully using chopsticks or a spoon. Serve hot.

Ingredients

1 clove garlic, minced

1 teaspoon ginger, minced

2 teaspoons light soy sauce

2 teaspoons dark soy sauce

1 teaspoon sesame oil

1 teaspoon sugar

pinch of salt

1 teaspoon cornflour

pinch of white pepper

4 tablespoons water

250 g (8 oz) minced pork

500 g (1 lb) soft tofu

2 spring onions

Meatloaf

This dish comes from the south of the United States. It is one of those wonderful old "comfort foods" that may well bring happy childhood memories flooding back in your parents' or grandparents' minds. You and your friends will also enjoy it! Serve it thickly sliced with mashed potato and ketchup or a spicy tomato sauce.

Ingredients

250 g (8 oz) minced beef

1 large onion, finely chopped

1 red pepper, finely chopped

500 ml (1 pint) ketchup

500 ml (1 pint) chopped tomatoes

2 eggs

200 g (7 oz) crackers, crushed

180 ml (¹/₃ pint) condensed milk

pinch brown sugar

1 Preheat the oven to 180°C/ 350°F/gas 4. Place the beef in a large bowl. Add the finely chopped onion and bell pepper.

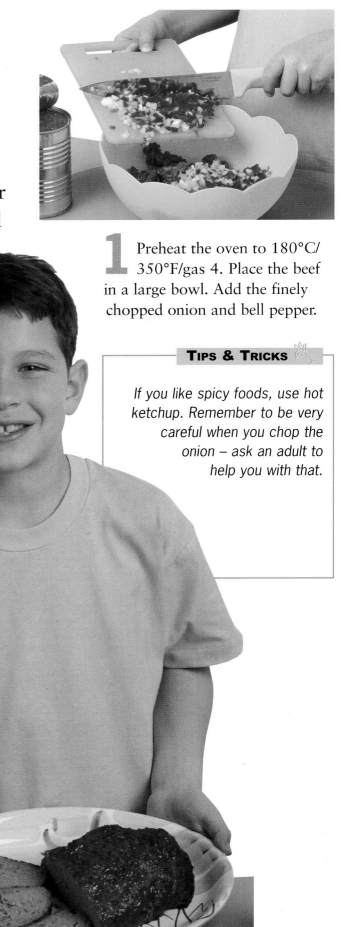

TIPS & TRICKS

If you like spicy foods, use hot ketchup. Remember to be very careful when you chop the onion – ask an adult to help you with that.

2 Stir in the chopped tomatoes and 375 ml (²/₃ pint) of the ketchup.

3 Beat the eggs and condensed milk in a small bowl and add to the meat mixture.

4 Add the crackers and mix with your hands until the mixture sticks together.

5 Transfer the meat mixture to a roasting pan and shape into a small loaf.

6 Bake for about 1 hour, or until the juices run clear.

7 Mix the remaining tomato sauce with brown sugar. Spread over the loaf and return to the oven for 20 minutes.

Utensils

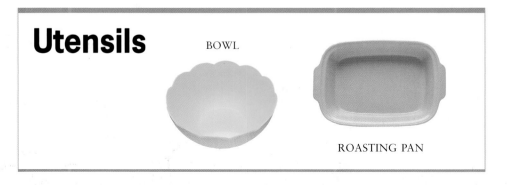

BOWL

ROASTING PAN

Barbecue Sauce

This all-American favourite tastes great on ribs, burgers, or hot dogs. You can also use it as a dip for French fries. It is served at parties all over the United States on 4th July, Independence Day. This celebration commemorates the American Declaration of Independence from Great Britain which was adopted in 1776.

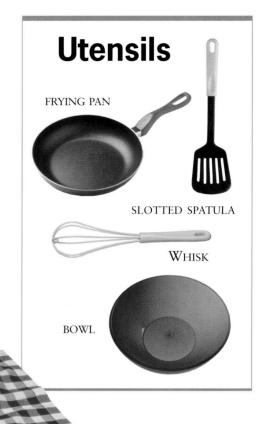

Utensils

FRYING PAN

SLOTTED SPATULA

WHISK

BOWL

TIPS & TRICKS

While cooking the sauce, make sure that the handle of the saucepan does not stick out. You might knock it onto yourself, or the floor, as you pass by.

1 Heat the butter in a frying pan over medium heat.

Ingredients

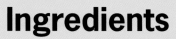

2 tablespoons butter
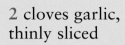

2 cloves garlic, thinly sliced

1 onion, thinly sliced

2 stalks celery, thinly sliced

4 tablespoons finely chopped parsley

2 tablespoons brown sugar

4 tablespoons Worcestershire sauce

2 tablespoons white wine vinegar

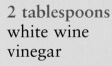

250 ml (½ pint) ketchup (spicy, if preferred)

125 ml (¼ pint) boiling water

2 Add the onion, garlic, celery, and parsley and sauté for about 5 minutes, or until the onions are transparent. Do not brown.

3 Sprinkle with the brown sugar.

4 Add the Worcestershire sauce, ketchup, vinegar, and water. Reduce the heat and simmer for 10 minutes, or until thickened.

Funny Fish

This dish tastes good even if you don't normally like fish. The strong flavour of the fish is softened a little by the potatoes and mayonnaise. It is also fun to make because you can model the "fish" mixture with your hands, sculpting it into the shape of a fish. Decorate your fish with the mayonnaise, adding the mouth, gills, scales, and tail.

Utensils

COLANDER

POTATO
MASHER

BOWL

76

1 Boil the potatoes in their skins in a pot of salted water for about 25 minutes, or until tender. Drain in a colander. When they have cooled a little, peel off the skins with your fingers.

2 Transfer the potatoes to a bowl and mash them using a potato masher. Use a plastic one, like the one shown here, or a simple wire masher.

Ingredients

750 g (1½ lb) potatoes

2 tablespoons finely chopped parsley

200 g (7 oz) tinned tuna, squashed with a fork

125 ml (¼ pint) mayonnaise, in a tube or painted on

dash of salt

1 clove garlic, finely chopped

3 Add the tuna, garlic, and parsley to the bowl with the potatoes. Mix well. Season with salt to taste.

4 Turn the mixture out on a large serving dish. You can use your hands to sculpt the mixture into the shape of a fish.

77

TIPS & TRICKS

Ask an adult to help move the pot of boiling water when draining potatoes. Always keep the mayonnaise in the refrigerator, especially just before you use it. Cold mayonnaise is easier to draw with.

5 Decorate the fish with the mayonnaise, squirting it out of the tube. Be creative by using a little parsley to add the fish's eye. You can draw in the gills, fins, and scales too.

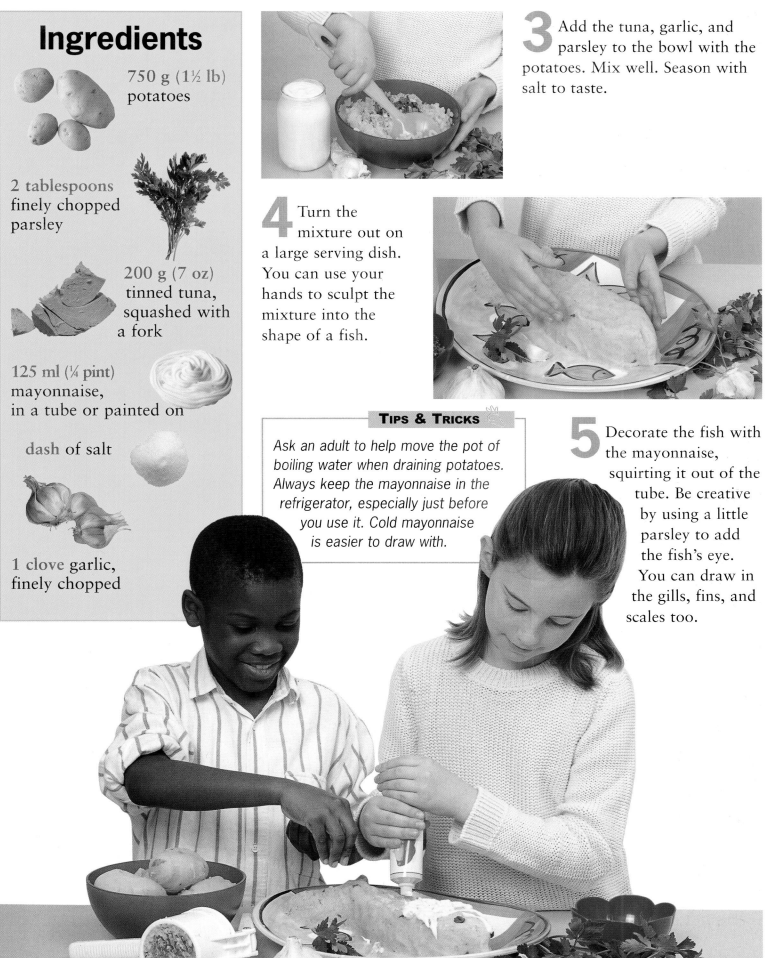

Butter, Lemon, and Parsley Sole

Sole is such a tasty fish that the ancient Romans called it *"solea jovis,"* or "Jupiter's sandal," in honour of one of their gods. Chefs have found many different ways of serving it. In French cuisine this recipe is called *"sole meunière,"* or miller's sole and is dipped in flour and sautéed in butter to make a tasty sauce.

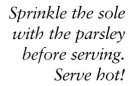

Sprinkle the sole with the parsley before serving. Serve hot!

TIPS & TRICKS

Turning the sole in the frying pan is a little difficult. Ask an adult to help you with this step. Be sure to take the pan off the heat while you do it. Any kind of small thin fish or fillet can be used for this recipe.

Depending on the size of your frying pan, add half of the butter for two sole or one quarter if only one sole will fit.

1 Place the flour in a large flat-bottomed bowl or plate. Dip the sole in it one at a time, making sure they are well coated on both sides.

2 Melt the butter in a nonstick frying pan over low heat. Add a drop of oil to the pan to prevent the butter from burning.

Ingredients

4 skinned sole fillets

6 tablespoons butter

1 lemon

6 tablespoons plain flour

2 tablespoons finely chopped parsley

salt

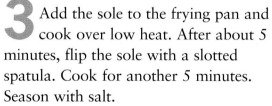

3 Add the sole to the frying pan and cook over low heat. After about 5 minutes, flip the sole with a slotted spatula. Cook for another 5 minutes. Season with salt.

4 While the sole is cooking, squeeze the lemon halves using a citrus juicer.

5 When the sole are almost cooked, pour half the lemon juice over them and cook for 1 more minute. Slip the sole onto a serving dish and cook the rest.

Utensils

FRYING PAN

SLOTTED SPATULA

CITRUS JUICER

Sweet and Sour Prawns

Chinese cuisine can be divided into four main regions. Most of the early Chinese immigrants to the West came from the Canton region so we know Cantonese recipes the best. The sweet and sour sauce in this recipe is a Cantonese sauce. It is also delicious with pork or chicken instead of the prawns.

1 Place the prawns in a bowl with 2 tablespoons of the soy sauce. Marinade for 30 minutes.

2 Beat the egg in a small bowl. Using chopsticks or your fingers dip the prawns into the egg.

3 Place 50 g (2 oz) of the cornflour on a plate. Dredge the prawns in the cornflour.

Ingredients

3 tablespoons light soy sauce

12 large prawns, shelled

75 g (2½ oz) cornflour

1 onion, cubed

1 egg

5 tablespoons vegetable oil

1 red pepper, diced

1 tablespoon sugar

1 tablespoon rice vinegar

pinch of salt

2 tablespoons tomato ketchup

2 tablespoons water

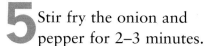

5 Stir fry the onion and pepper for 2–3 minutes.

TIPS & TRICKS

You can adjust the sauce by adding more or less sugar and vinegar. More sugar makes the sauce sweeter, while more vinegar makes it more sour. If you do not have rice vinegar, use half a tablespoon of lemon juice instead. If you use pork or chicken, cut the meat into cubes and prepare in the same way as the prawns.

4 Heat the oil in the wok. Add the prawns and cook until they turn an orangey-pink colour. Be careful you don't get splashed by the oil – ask an adult to help you. Use a slotted spoon to remove the prawns. Place them on paper towels. Pour out most of the oil, except about 1 tablespoon.

Utensils

BOWLS

CHOPSTICKS

WOK OR
FRYING PAN

6 Place the cooked prawns back in the wok and mix well.

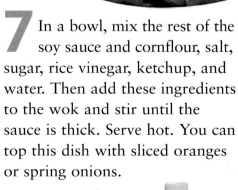

7 In a bowl, mix the rest of the soy sauce and cornflour, salt, sugar, rice vinegar, ketchup, and water. Then add these ingredients to the wok and stir until the sauce is thick. Serve hot. You can top this dish with sliced oranges or spring onions.

Tuna, Egg, and Tomato Salad

This healthy, colourful salad is easy to prepare and requires no cooking. Served with freshly baked French bread, this salad makes a nutritious lunch or snack. It comes from Nice, a beautiful city on the Mediterranean Sea in the south of France. Many fish dishes are unique to this region. The ingredients can be changed so that if you do not like onions, for example, you can replace them with another herb or vegetable.

1 Wash the vegetables and dry them thoroughly. Slice the red pepper across the middle and remove the seeds and core. Slice it into thin, round strips.

2 Peel and slice the cucumber into thin pieces. Cut the tomatoes into thin wedges and the onion into thin wheels. Place the lettuce leaves in a salad bowl.

Utensils

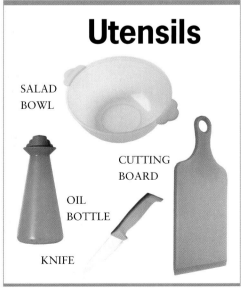

SALAD BOWL

CUTTING BOARD

OIL BOTTLE

KNIFE

4 Sprinkle with a little salt and drizzle with the oil. Use salad tongs to toss the ingredients. Be sure to do this carefully so that the eggs do not break up.

3 Peel the eggs and cut them in quarters lengthwise. Add the eggs and the other ingredients on top of the lettuce leaves.

TIPS & TRICKS

Be very careful with the knife when you are chopping the vegetables. Ask an adult to help. Hold the knife firmly by the handle and use your other hand to hold the vegetables. Always watch what you are doing, and make sure that your fingertips stay well away from the blade of the knife.

Ingredients

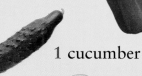

10 fresh large lettuce leaves

1 red pepper

1 cucumber

1 red onion

2 ripe salad tomatoes

2 hard-boiled eggs

200 g (7 oz) tinned tuna in olive oil

12 black olives

salt

3 tablespoons extra virgin olive oil

Easy Potato Knishes

These delicious potato puffs are a traditional Jewish dish. Jewish immigrants from Eastern Europe brought their recipes with them when they went to the United States. Nowadays knishes are especially associated with New York where street vendors sell them at busy corners all over the city. Our recipe is easier than most because it doesn't have the pastry casing.

Utensils

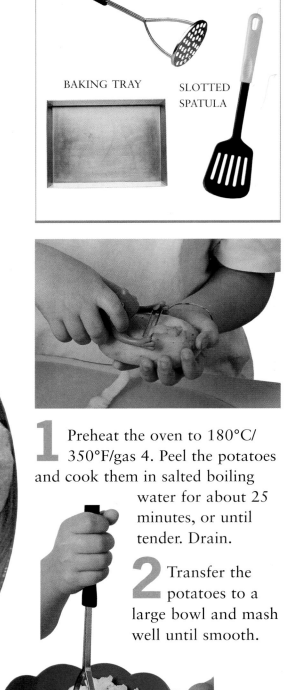

POTATO MASHER

BOWL

BAKING TRAY

SLOTTED SPATULA

1 Preheat the oven to 180°C/ 350°F/gas 4. Peel the potatoes and cook them in salted boiling water for about 25 minutes, or until tender. Drain.

2 Transfer the potatoes to a large bowl and mash well until smooth.

3 Add the eggs one at a time and mix until well blended.

4 Stir in the potato starch. The mixture should be dry enough to shape into balls with your hands. Add more starch if needed.

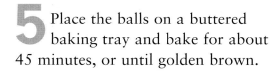

5 Place the balls on a buttered baking tray and bake for about 45 minutes, or until golden brown.

Ingredients

6 large potatoes

½ teaspoon salt

6 eggs, lightly beaten

6 tablespoons potato starch

Pinto Beans with Tomato and Bacon

Beans are native to Mexico and are one of the country's most common foods. There are many recipes with beans as the main ingredient. In Mexico, beans are traditionally cooked in large clay pots. These pots give the beans a special flavour. You can also use a pressure cooker or a pan with a tight lid. Dried pinto beans need to be soaked overnight before they are used.

1 Carefully sort through the dried beans. Throw away any beans that are wrinkled or cracked. Pick out any small stones.

2 Place the beans in a bowl and cover with water. Soak them overnight. Afterwards, drain the water and place the beans in a pressure cooker.

Utensils

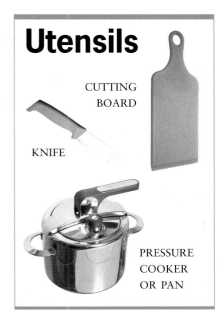

CUTTING
BOARD

KNIFE

PRESSURE
COOKER
OR PAN

4 Cook for about 1 hour, or until the beans are plump and soft. Check often to make sure there is still water covering the beans. Ask an adult to help you when raising the lid.

3 Chop the garlic and bacon and mix them with the beans. Add the crushed tomatoes, salt, and just enough water to cover the beans. Put on the lid and bring to the boil.

Easy refried beans
If there are any beans left over: fry an additional 4 to 5 slices of chopped bacon. Add the beans and mash. Serve on tacos, chalupas, or as a side dish.

Ingredients

250 g (8 oz) dried pinto beans

1 clove garlic

3 slices bacon

1 tin (400 g/14 oz) crushed tomatoes

½ teaspoon salt

cold water, as required

TIPS & TRICKS

A pressure cooker is a pot with a locking lid and a valve for steam to escape from. Food is cooked quickly in these pots. If you do not have one in your kitchen, just use a large, deep saucepan with a tight-fitting lid. Beans cooked in this type of pot will take about 2 hours to cook.

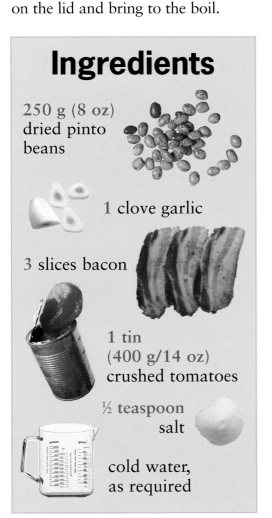

French Cherry Tart

This tasty dessert is quick to make and to eat! It is a speciality from the central French region of Limousin. Its French name – *Clafoutis* – comes from a dialect word *clafir*, which means "to fill." The original recipe uses whole cherries with their stones, but it is a good idea to remove the stones before you begin, or buy cherries with the stones already removed.

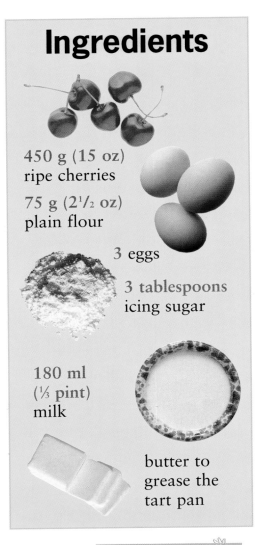

Ingredients

450 g (15 oz) ripe cherries

75 g (2½ oz) plain flour

3 eggs

3 tablespoons icing sugar

180 ml (⅓ pint) milk

butter to grease the tart pan

Serve the tart straight from the oven with vanilla ice cream or let it cool and serve with whipped cream.

TIPS & TRICKS

If cherries are not in season, replace them with the same quantity of any kind of berry or fruit used in cooking. Always use protective oven gloves when putting things into or taking them out of the oven.

1 Preheat the oven to 190°C/ 375°F/gas 5. Wash the cherries under cold running water, drain well, and pat dry. Remove the stems and the stones.

Utensils

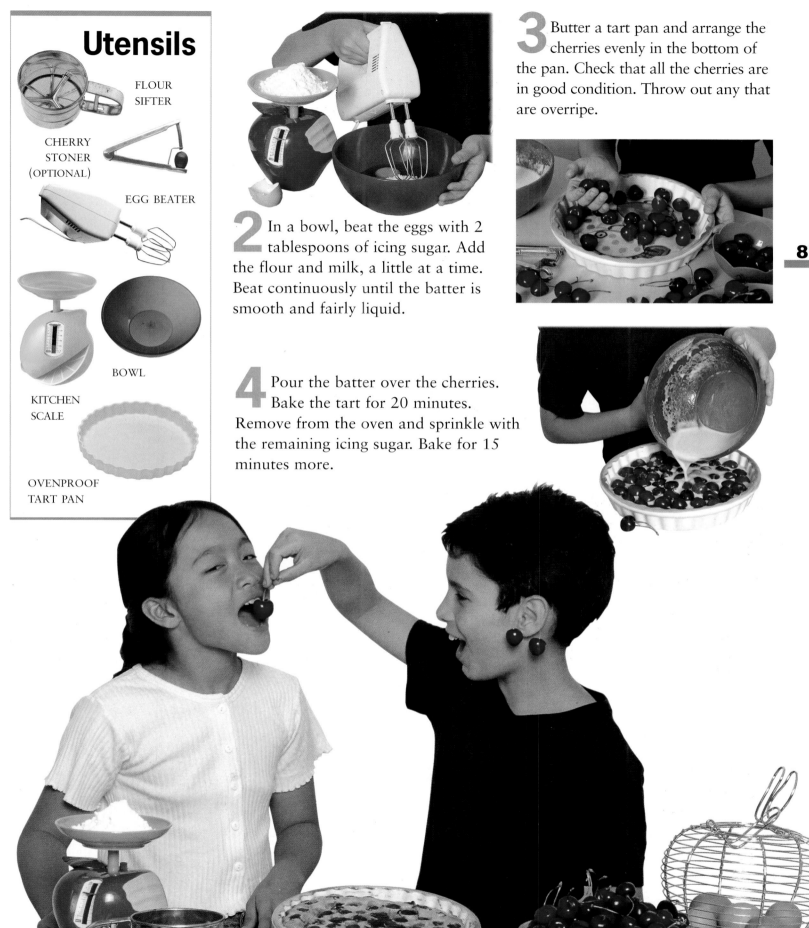

FLOUR SIFTER

CHERRY STONER (OPTIONAL)

EGG BEATER

BOWL

KITCHEN SCALE

OVENPROOF TART PAN

2 In a bowl, beat the eggs with 2 tablespoons of icing sugar. Add the flour and milk, a little at a time. Beat continuously until the batter is smooth and fairly liquid.

3 Butter a tart pan and arrange the cherries evenly in the bottom of the pan. Check that all the cherries are in good condition. Throw out any that are overripe.

4 Pour the batter over the cherries. Bake the tart for 20 minutes. Remove from the oven and sprinkle with the remaining icing sugar. Bake for 15 minutes more.

French Strawberry Tart

France is the third largest producer of strawberries in the world. It is not surprising then that the French were the inventors of this delicious tart. Grown in the Rhone Valley, Brittany, and in other areas of France, strawberries are full of vitamins and are very good for you.

Ingredients

375 g (12 oz) plain flour

125 g (4 oz) butter

2 egg yolks

5 tablespoons sugar

200 g (7 oz) strawberry jam

1 kg (2 lb) clean, fresh strawberries

1 kg (2 lb) dried beans

1 Sift the flour into a bowl. Add the butter and work it in with your fingers until the mixture is the consistency of breadcrumbs. Stir in the egg yolks, then shape the pastry into a ball. Wrap it in plastic wrap and place in the refrigerator for about 30 minutes. Preheat the oven to 180°C/350°F/ gas 4.

5 Dilute the jam with 2–3 tablespoons of warm water. Use a new, clean pastry brush to "paint" the top of the strawberries with the jam. Remove from the pan and serve at room temperature with ice cream or whipped cream.

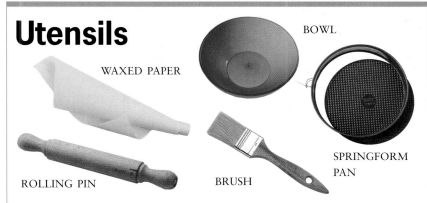

Utensils

BOWL

WAXED PAPER

SPRINGFORM PAN

ROLLING PIN

BRUSH

2 Sprinkle flour on a rolling pin and roll the dough out on a floured work surface until it is about 5 mm (¼ inch) thick.

4 Remove the baked pastry shell from the oven and discard the paper and beans. Arrange the strawberries, pointed end facing upward on the pastry in the pan.

3 Use the dough to line a buttered and floured 26 cm (10 inch) diameter springform pan. Cover with a sheet of waxed paper and fill with the dried beans. Bake for about 20 minutes, or until pale golden brown.

TIPS & TRICKS

Be sure to use a springform pan, otherwise it will be hard to get the tart out of the baking pan without breaking it. If strawberries are out of season, replace them with the same quantity of raspberries.

Chocolate Mousse

Soft, fluffy, and sweet, mousse is almost pure chocolate and will be a favourite with your family and friends. Chocolate mousse is one of the easiest and most common French desserts to make. It became a popular treat in the 1970s with the introduction of *nouvelle cuisine* (a light, modern approach to traditional French cooking). The best part about this recipe is cleaning up afterward and licking the spoons!

1 Put the chocolate in a small saucepan with the milk and then put the saucepan into a larger pan of cold water. Place over medium heat, and stir until the chocolate melts.

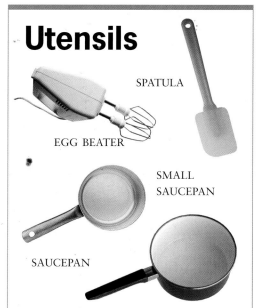

2 Beat the egg yolks with the sugar. Stir into the chocolate and cook until the mixture registers 70°C (160°F) on an 'instant-read' thermometer.

Utensils

SPATULA

EGG BEATER

SMALL SAUCEPAN

SAUCEPAN

3 Beat the egg whites with a dash of salt until they form stiff peaks. Fold the beaten egg whites into the chocolate, taking care that the egg whites do not unstiffen.

4 Beat the cream with an electric or hand held beater until thick. Fold it carefully into the chocolate and egg mixture.

TIPS & TRICKS

When melting the chocolate, be sure to place the saucepans on back burners and keep a firm grip on the handle as you stir. Do not over-whip the cream in step 4, or it will become the same texture as butter.

5 Transfer the mousse mixture into individual dessert dishes or one large serving bowl. Leave in the refrigerator for at least 4 hours before serving. Add whipped cream if desired.

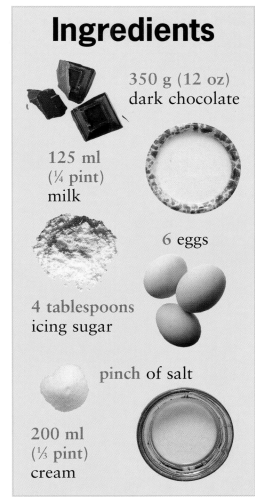

Ingredients

350 g (12 oz) dark chocolate

125 ml (¼ pint) milk

6 eggs

4 tablespoons icing sugar

pinch of salt

200 ml (⅓ pint) cream

Chocolate Cream Puffs

Also known as profiteroles, you might have seen this rich-looking dessert in the windows of bakeries many times. Now you can make it at home. The cream puff pastry cases are made with choux pastry and are quite difficult to prepare at home. We suggest that you buy them already made. Then fill them with ice cream, dip them in chocolate, and decorate with whipped cream.

Ingredients

200 g (7 oz) dark chocolate

300 g (10 oz) ready-made cream puff cases

300 g (10 oz) vanilla ice cream

250 ml (½ pint) whipping cream

1 Use a knife to break up the chocolate. Put the chocolate in a small saucepan and then put the saucepan in a larger pan of cold water. Place over medium heat, and stir until the chocolate melts.

TIPS & TRICKS

Take the ice cream out of the freezer just before you begin to fill the cream puffs. If you take it out too early it will melt while you work. You can also try filling the cream puffs with vanilla custard or whipped cream instead of the ice cream. You can also add fruit sauce on top of the dessert.

2 Make a small hole in each cream puff case. Using a pastry chef's syringe, fill each one with ice cream.

3 Arrange the filled cream puffs on a round plate one on top of the other in a pyramid shape. Use a little of the chocolate to stick them together.

Place attractive blobs or swirls of cream all over the cream puff pyramid.

4 Pour the remaining chocolate over the top so that it runs down the sides. Beat the cream until it is thick. Fill the syringe with the whipped cream and decorate the stack of cream puffs.

Utensils

EGG BEATER

KNIFE

PASTRY CHEF'S SYRINGE

SPATULA

Crème Brûlée

This delicious baked vanilla custard is called *Crème brûlée*. The name means "burnt custard" in French, but this dessert is not actually burnt. The brown sugar when placed under a grill forms a melt-in-your-mouth crust, which combines well with the creamy vanilla custard underneath. To really enjoy crème brûlée, serve it while it is still a bit warm.

Ingredients

7 egg yolks

150 g (5 oz) sugar

500 ml (1 pint) fresh cream

100 ml (4 fl oz) milk

4 tablespoons brown sugar

1 Preheat the oven to 180°C/ 350°F/gas 4. In a bowl, beat the separated egg yolks with the sugar until they are pale and creamy.

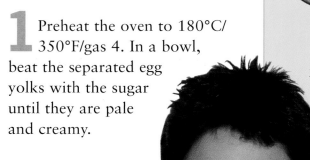

TIPS & TRICKS

Ask an adult to help you place the roasting pan filled with custard in the oven. You must be careful not to spill water in the oven. When checking to see if it is cooked, and when broiling the sugar, remember to wear thick oven gloves.

2 Heat the cream and milk together. Just before they boil, remove from heat and pour them into the egg and sugar mixture, beating continuously.

To test whether the baked custard is cooked, insert a cake tester or toothpick into the custard. If it comes out dry and clean, the custard is ready.

Utensils

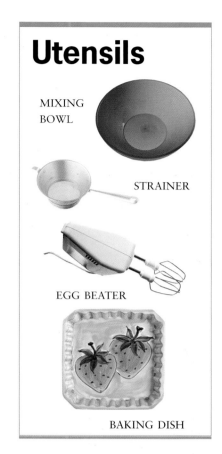

MIXING BOWL

STRAINER

EGG BEATER

BAKING DISH

3 Filter the mixture using a strainer.

4 Pour the mixture into a buttered ovenproof dish. Put the dish in a larger dish or pan, such as a roasting pan, filled with cold water. Place both dishes the oven and cook for 1 hour. Ask an adult to help you carry the heavy pans.

5 Remove from the oven and set aside to cool. Sprinkle with the brown sugar and place under a preheated grill for 5 minutes until the sugar is browned and crisp.

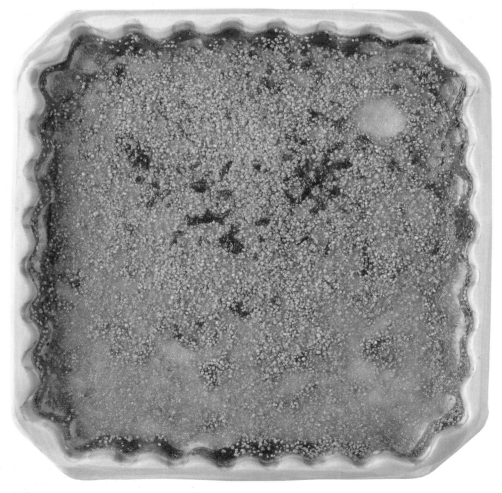

Pumpkin Pie

There is an old saying that goes "As American as pumpkin pie," which explains the origins of this American dessert very well. It was invented by the Pilgrims, who learned to grow and cook pumpkins from the Native Americans. In its earliest version, to celebrate the first Thanksgivings, it was made by hollowing out a pumpkin, filling it with milk, and baking it whole.

Utensils

BOWL

ROLLING PIN

SPATULA

PIE DISH

Ingredients

3 large eggs

500 g (1 lb) freshly cooked or tinned pumpkin puree

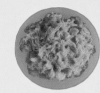

375 ml (⅔ pint) single cream

150 g (5 oz) sugar

½ teaspoon each ground nutmeg and allspice

1 teaspoon each ground cinnamon and ginger

250 g (8 oz) short-crust pastry

½ teaspoon salt

whipped cream to serve

TIPS & TRICKS

You can refrigerate this pie for up to 1 day before serving. Remember to use thick oven gloves to remove the hot pie plate from the oven. Ask an adult to help you.

1 Preheat the oven to 190°C/375°F/gas 5. Beat the eggs in a large bowl until frothy. Add the pumpkin, cream, and sugar.

2 Stir in the cinnamon, ginger, nutmeg, allspice, and salt.

3 Roll the pastry out on a floured work surface to 5 mm (¼ inch) thick.

4 Press the pastry into a pie dish, making a fluted edge.

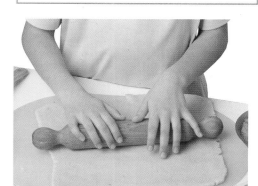

99

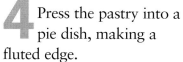

5 Pour the pumpkin filling into the pastry base. Bake for about 35 minutes, or until the centre of the pie is set but still slightly quivery.

Pavlova

This delicious meringue cake is a typically Australian cake. It was named in honour of the visit of Anna Pavlova, the famous Russian ballerina, to Australia and New Zealand in the early 1900's. Try melting chocolate and varying the fruit for extra-special occasions.

Ingredients

6 egg whites

300 g (10 oz) sugar

1½ tablespoons cornflour

1½ teaspoons white vinegar

250 ml (½ pint) whipped cream

2 kiwi fruit, sliced

250 g (8 oz) sliced strawberries

1 Preheat the oven to 130°C/250°F/gas ½. Cover two baking sheets with parchment paper. Set a plate upside-down and use a pencil to draw out two 20 cm (8 inch) circles.

TIPS & TRICKS

Make sure that you use a clean, dry bowl to beat the egg whites. Any moisture or residue may cause the meringue not to form stiff, glossy peaks. To create extra glossy peaks, beat the whites at medium speed, gradually add the sugar then beat at high speed.

2 Beat the egg whites and sugar until stiff peaks form. Fold in the cornflour and vinegar. Reserve one-third of the meringue and spread the rest over the paper circles.

3 Drop spoonfuls of meringue around the edge of one of the meringue circles.

4 Bake for about 1 hour and 30 minutes, or until the meringues are crisp and dry. Cool the meringues in the oven with the door ajar.

Utensils

SPATULA

BAKING TRAY

BOWL

MIXER

PARCHMENT PAPER

5 Cover the top and sides of the plain meringue with whipped cream. Decorate with half the kiwi and strawberries.

6 Place the meringue with the decorations on top. Decorate with the remaining kiwis, strawberries, and a little whipped cream.

Ladybird Birthday Cake

The tradition of making special cakes to celebrate birthdays is believed to have started many years ago in Germany, where people began adding small surprises to their cakes. The object found in the cake was supposed to represent their future. A coin meant wealth while a thimble meant that you would never marry!

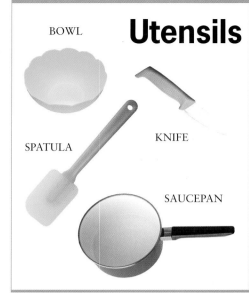

Utensils

BOWL

SPATULA

KNIFE

SAUCEPAN

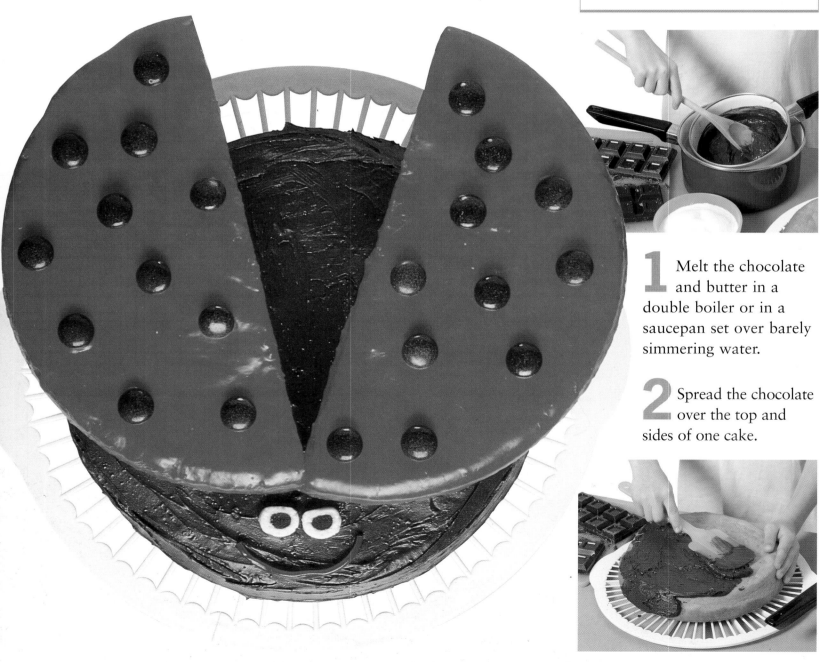

1 Melt the chocolate and butter in a double boiler or in a saucepan set over barely simmering water.

2 Spread the chocolate over the top and sides of one cake.

Ingredients

180 g (6 oz) butter

200 g (7 oz) milk chocolate

2 round 28 cm (10 inch) sponge cakes

375 ml ready-made frosting, coloured with red food colouring

dark-coloured chocolate or sweets

3 Slice the remaining cake in half and spread the top and sides of each half with the red vanilla frosting.

4 Place the red frosted cakes on top of the chocolate frosted cake to resemble wings.

5 Decorate with the sweets as desired.

TIPS & TRICKS

To really enjoy making this cake, you could make a sponge cake yourself and decorate it in any manner that you like. Vary the decoration.

Cheesecake

Cheesecake is served at the Jewish festival of Shavuot, which marks harvest in the farming year. As part of the tradition, foods containing milk and cheese are eaten in celebration. Serve this creamy cheesecake as is or with a melted fruit jelly glaze or chopped fresh fruit.

1 Preheat the oven to 180°C/350°F/gas 4. Place the biscuit crumbs and half the sugar in a large bowl. Add the butter.

2 Press the crumb mixture into the base of a 28 cm (10 inch) springform pan. Bake the crumb base for 10 minutes.

Utensils

ELECTRIC MIXER

SPRINGFORM PAN

SPATULA

BOWL

104

TIPS & TRICKS

Remove the springform sides first, followed by the bottom. If the cheesecake sticks, serve on the pan bottom.

Ingredients

125 g (4 oz) digestive biscuits, crumbed

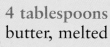

4 tablespoons sugar

4 tablespoons butter, melted

1 kg (2 lb) cream cheese, softened

3 tablespoons plain flour

4 eggs

250 ml (½ pint) sour cream

2 teaspoons vanilla extract

3 Beat the cream cheese, remaining sugar, and flour in a large bowl with an electric mixer until creamy.

4 Add the eggs, beating until just blended. Beat in the sour cream and vanilla.

5 Pour the filling into the baked crust and bake for 1 hour. Cool the cheesecake in the oven with the door ajar.

6 Remove the pan sides and refrigerate for at least 2 hours before serving.

Pancakes

Pancakes are served on Shrove Tuesday of the Christian calendar, to use up all rich items before the 40-day fast of Lent. Lent is the time before Easter when Christians repent their sins and receive forgiveness. Serve these pancakes sprinkled with sugar and lemon juice or rolled up with jam.

Utensils

WHISK

SLOTTED SPATULA

BOWL

FRYING PAN

1 Sift the flour and salt into a large bowl.

2 Gradually add the milk, stirring constantly so that no lumps form.

3 Beat the eggs in a large bowl with a whisk. Gradually add the dry ingredients, whisking constantly.

4 Melt 1 tablespoon of the butter in a frying pan. Then add a ladleful of the batter, tilting the pan so that the batter covers the bottom completely.

107

TIPS & TRICKS

Melt the butter before adding the batter to the frying pan. It is best to use a nonstick pan to make pancakes as they may stick to the bottom.

5 Place over medium heat and cook until the underside is golden brown. Flip and brown the other side.

6 Spread each pancake with jam and roll up carefully.

Ingredients

125 g (4 oz) plain flour

pinch of salt

375 ml (⅔ pint) milk

3 eggs

4 tablespoons butter

250 g (8 oz) fruit jam

Chocolate Cake

If you get cravings for chocolate, this is the perfect recipe for you! When eaten in small quantities chocolate is not bad for you. It is not even true that it will give you pimples. The latest research shows that chocolate is a mood enhancer, which means that it makes you feel good. So don't feel guilty about loving this cake!

108

Ingredients

200 g (7 oz) dark chocolate

90 g (3oz) butter

250 ml (1 cup) caster sugar

4 egg whites

pinch of salt

2 tablespoons plain flour

250 ml (½ pint) whipped cream in a piping bag

1 Preheat the oven to 150°C/300°F/gas 3. Place a large saucepan of water over medium heat. Put the chocolate and butter in a smaller pan and place it in the larger one. Cook, stirring all the time, until they have melted.

TIPS & TRICKS

Place the cake in the oven on the middle rack. Don't open the door during the first 20 minutes of cooking time, or your cake may go flat. Ask an adult to take the cake out of the oven or use thick oven gloves to protect your hands.

2 Remove the saucepan from the heat. Add the sugar and stir until it has dissolved. Gradually add the flour, stirring until well mixed. Set aside to cool.

Utensils

PIPING BAG

MIXING SPOON

SAUCEPAN

SPATULA

3 Separate the eggs and beat the egg whites until stiff using a hand beater or an electric mixer. Add salt first so the eggs will be ready sooner.

4 When the chocolate mixture is lukewarm, carefully mix in the egg whites. Use a spatula to lift up the chocolate mixture and gently blend in the egg whites.

5 Grease and flour a 28 cm (10 inch) diameter springform pan and pour the mixture into it. Bake for about 25 minutes. The cake should have a light crust but still be soft inside. To test if the cake is cooked, poke a toothpick into the middle; if it comes out clean the cake is ready. Remove from the oven and turn out onto a wire rack to cool.

6 When the cake is cool, decorate it with the whipped cream.

Tiramisù

This creamy chocolate dessert comes from Italy. It is so good that four different Italian regions – Lombardy, Emilia-Romagna, Veneto, and Tuscany – all claim to have invented it! It is fun to make and tasty to eat. When you serve it, your friends and family will think you are a gourmet chef. The name of this dessert is pronounced with the accent on the last syllable and means "pick me up."

TIPS & TRICKS

If your local supermarket or grocery store does not have mascarpone cheese, use the same quantity of cream cheese in its place. This dessert needs to be chilled for at least two hours in the refrigerator, so remember to start early. If you do not like the taste of coffee, replace it with the same quantity of raspberry syrup.

Ingredients

5 eggs, separated

150 g (5 oz) sugar

500 g (1 lb) mascarpone cheese

about 30 sponge fingers

250 ml (1 cup) strong black coffee

200 g (7 oz) dark chocolate, grated

1 tablespoon unsweetened cocoa powder

Utensils

EGG BEATER

MIXING BOWL

SPATULA

5 Put the cocoa in a sifter and sift evenly over the top to finish. Place in the refrigerator for at least two hours before serving.

1 Separate the eggs. Beat the yolks and sugar. Cook until the mixture registers 70°C (160°F) on an instant-read thermometer. Let cool and stir in the mascarpone.

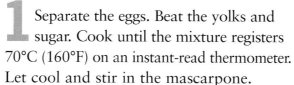

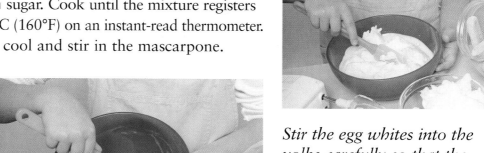

Stir the egg whites into the yolks carefully so that the mixture stays light and fluffy.

2 Beat the egg whites until they form a stiff mixture. Carefully stir the beaten egg whites into the egg yolks and mascarpone until well mixed.

Dip the sponge fingers into the coffee quickly so that they absorb a little, but do not become too soggy.

3 Cover the bottom of a serving dish with a layer of the mixture. Dip some sponge fingers into the coffee and then place them in a layer over the cream.

Use the spatula to spread the cream over the sponge fingers in an even layer.

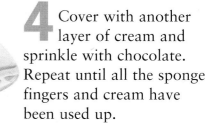

4 Cover with another layer of cream and sprinkle with chocolate. Repeat until all the sponge fingers and cream have been used up.

Ice Cream with Hot Fudge Sauce

Ice cream with hot chocolate sauce is one of the most delicious ways to finish a meal. Some believe ice cream was invented in China, around 3000 BC. The ancient Chinese mixed snow with fruit and honey and, in time, ice cream became popular all over the world. Italian pastry chefs perfected the art of making ice cream in the 1500s and called it *gelato*.

TIPS & TRICKS

If you do not have an ice cream maker, place the mixture in a freezer proof bowl and place in the freezer. After two hours, stir quickly and put it back in the freezer. Repeat twice.

1 Separate the eggs. In a mixing bowl, beat the egg yolks and the sugar with a whisk until they are pale and creamy.

Utensils

WHISK

MIXING SPOON

SAUCEPAN

ICE CREAM MAKER

Ingredients

4 egg yolks

100 g (3 oz) sugar

250 ml (½ pint) milk

200 ml (⅓ pint) cream

250 g (8 oz) dark chocolate

2 tablespoons butter

2 Add the milk and then half the cream gradually to the mixture, beating all the time until they have been completely absorbed.

3 Pour the mixture into the ice cream maker and follow the instructions to make the ice cream. If you do not have an ice cream maker see the Tips & Tricks box for instructions on how to make ice cream by hand.

4 When the ice cream is ready, place the chocolate, butter, and remaining cream in a small saucepan. Fill a larger saucepan half full of water and put the smaller one inside. Place over medium heat until the ingredients have all melted together. Put the ice cream in a serving bowl and pour the chocolate sauce over top.

Rice Pudding

Rice pudding is a traditional Mexican dessert. The pudding can be served chilled or while it is still warm with brown sugar. An exciting way is to cook the pudding until it is very stodgy. Roll it into balls and fry them until golden brown. Sprinkle the balls with cinnamon and sugar and serve warm.

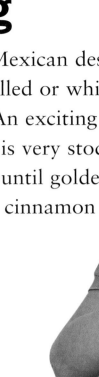

1 Combine the rice, evaporated milk, sugar, and egg yolks in a saucepan over a medium heat. Stir.

2 Add the vanilla essence, raisins, and spices. Simmer for 5 minutes over a low heat. Remove from the heat.

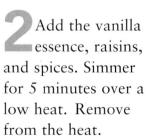

3 Beat the egg whites with a mixer until they are stiff. Fold the whites carefully into the rice mixture.

4 Spoon the mixture into bowls. Sprinkle with the cinnamon and place in the refrigerator for at least 2 hours. Serve when chilled.

Utensils

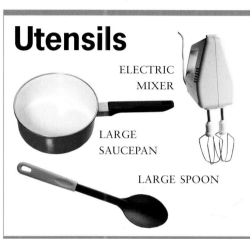

ELECTRIC MIXER

LARGE SAUCEPAN

LARGE SPOON

Ingredients

250 g (8 oz) cooked rice

500 ml (1 pint) evaporated milk

GLORIA
LECHE
EVAPORADA

150 g (5 oz) sugar

250 g (8 oz) raisins

3 eggs, separated

1 teaspoon vanilla extract

¼ teaspoon ground cinnamon

¼ teaspoon ground nutmeg

TIPS & TRICKS

Separating eggs takes practice. Crack the egg over the bowl. Gently pour the egg into half of the shell without breaking the yolk (the yellow part). Allow the white to slide into the bowl. Repeat until all the yolks and whites are separated. Put the yolks in a separate container from the whites.

Egg Custard Tarts

Egg custard tarts are the perfect way to finish a Chinese meal. The egg custard tarts can be made with either flaky or shortcrust pastry, although the traditional tart is made with a flaky pastry. Choose the pastry you think tastes better.

Ingredients

2 large eggs

3 egg yolks

250 g (8 oz) sugar

250 ml (¹/₂ pint) milk

125 ml (¹/₄ pint) single cream

1 packet ready-made frozen pastry (flaky or shortcrust)

1 Preheat the oven to 150°C/ 300°F/gas 2.

Utensils

LARGE BOWL

ROUND PASTRY CUTTER

INDIVIDUAL TART TINS

WHISK

2 Combine the egg yolks and whole eggs in a jug or bowl. Beat them slowly with the whisk.

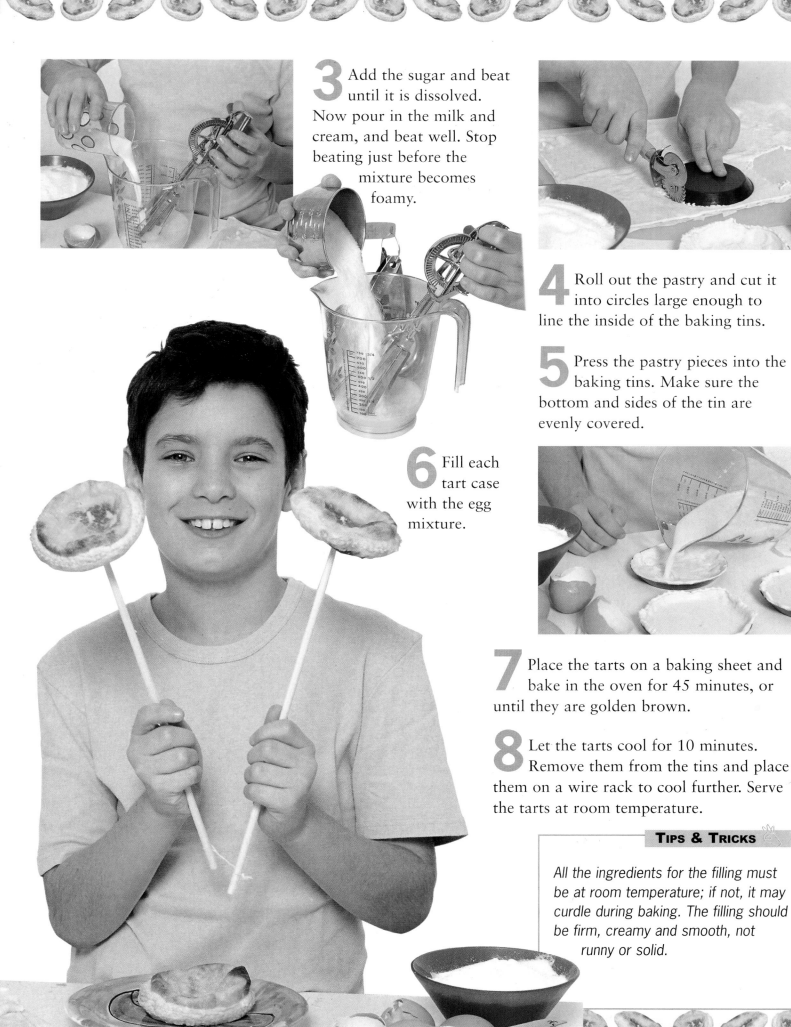

3 Add the sugar and beat until it is dissolved. Now pour in the milk and cream, and beat well. Stop beating just before the mixture becomes foamy.

4 Roll out the pastry and cut it into circles large enough to line the inside of the baking tins.

5 Press the pastry pieces into the baking tins. Make sure the bottom and sides of the tin are evenly covered.

6 Fill each tart case with the egg mixture.

7 Place the tarts on a baking sheet and bake in the oven for 45 minutes, or until they are golden brown.

8 Let the tarts cool for 10 minutes. Remove them from the tins and place them on a wire rack to cool further. Serve the tarts at room temperature.

TIPS & TRICKS

All the ingredients for the filling must be at room temperature; if not, it may curdle during baking. The filling should be firm, creamy and smooth, not runny or solid.

Index